The Morally Beautiful

Reflections on Moral Nobility

Douglas P. McManaman

DPM Publishing
Aurora, Ontario

DPM also publishes its books in a variety of electronic formats.

Library and Archives Canada Cataloguing in Publication

McManaman, Douglas

The Morally Beautiful: Reflections on Moral Nobility

Aurora, Ontario: DPM Publishing. 2018

ISBN: 978-0-9948233-5-9

Cover by Jennifer Johnson, 2018.

This book is dedicated in gratitude to Dr. Joseph M. Boyle Jr.

Table of Contents

1. Introduction

In my Father's house, there are many mansions.

When I hear this reading (Jn 14, 1-12), I often think of the time I visited Trinity Retreat house in Larchmont, New York, a center that was, at the time, run by Father Benedict Groeschel. Between talks we'd have time to go for walks around Larchmont, one of the richest neighborhoods in the United States. The houses are magnificent; each one is different, very large, and very beautiful to look at. Many of the big new mansions going up here in Southern Ontario are magnificent as well; sometimes I will drive through these new developments and dream about living in one of those stone mansions, and then I would think of this verse: "In my Father's house, there are many mansions". I often wonder whether or not I would be any happier living in a place like that. For a while, no doubt, but once the novelty wears off, would I really be any happier than I am now if we made that kind of money and lived like that? Life would be more convenient, but would it necessarily be a happier life? I have my doubts.

My spiritual director grew up in Brooklyn, and he too visited Trinity Retreat house, and he recalls walking around the Yacht Club, enjoying the boats, the water, and the mansions. He asked his friend who was with him: If you had your choice, in which mansion would you want to live? And he would reply: "Oh, if I had my choice, I'd want to live in that one over there". My spiritual director then said: "Well if I had my choice, I'd want to live in that one over there", pointing to one in the opposite direction. Just a few feet away from them, sitting on a park bench, was an older lady, and as he said those words, she perked up and said: "No, you would not want to live in that house over there. I live in that house over there, and that's why I'm sitting here".

This verse, "In my Father's house, there are many mansions" clearly does not mean literally mansion or house. St. John of the Cross, the great 16th century Spanish mystic, wrote in the first line of his famous poem: *The Ascent of Mount Carmel*:

> On a dark night, Kindled in love with yearnings – oh, happy chance! –
> I went forth without being observed, My house being now at rest **(En una noche oscura, Con ansias, en amores inflamada, oh dichosa ventura! Sali sin ser notada, Estando ya mi casa sosegada.)**

The house he refers to is his entire soul, which includes the passions, the intellect and will. When someone does something seriously wrong, like murder or fraud, and gets away with it, others will often say things like: "How can you stand to look at yourself in the mirror?" or "How can you live with yourself?" No matter how much money you have, if you can't live with yourself, if you don't like what you have become, then it makes no difference what kind of a house you live in or how large a piece of property you have, because the house that Jesus is talking about is the interior dwelling place of your own soul, and either God dwells there or he does not.

In the book of Revelations, we read: "You keep saying, "I am so rich and secure that I want for nothing." Little do you realize how wretched you are, how pitiable and poor, how blind and naked! Take my advice. Buy from me gold refined by fire if you would be truly rich. Buy white garments in which to be clothed, if the shame of your nakedness is to be covered. Buy ointment to smear on your eyes, if you would see once more. Whoever is dear to me I reprove and chastise. Be earnest about it, therefore. Repent!

'Here I stand, knocking at the door. If anyone hears me calling and opens the door, I will enter his house and have supper with him, and he with me". (Rev 3, 17-20)

If Christ is not there dining with us, then we are alone, no matter how many people we have surrounding us. The mansion he speaks about in this gospel reading, the dwelling place, is the heart. The heart is really one's moral identity; it refers to one's moral character, the kind of person that you and I have made ourselves to be by the moral choices that we have made in life and continue to make every day. Every time we make a morally significant choice, in part we shape a moral identity. We are building our eternal mansion here and now through those very choices. If I choose to steal, I become a thief—that's who I am, even if no one knows about it; if I choose to lie, I become a liar, and if I choose to kill, I am a killer, etc.

I am reminded of a film produced years ago by TV Ontario, a film on Euthanasia in Holland. In it, a doctor was interviewed who would euthanize patients if they requested it. He said he had to take off his white coat every time he would euthanize a patient, and he didn't know why. The reason, of course, is that at that moment, he's no longer a doctor; a doctor heals, cares for his patients, keeps them as comfortable as possible, he does not murder them. The word medical comes from the Latin *medicor*, which means 'to heal', to 'make whole'. Subconsciously, he knows this, which is why he takes off his white coat.

We are building our mansion here, in this life. What will our mansion look like? Will it be an ugly, small, dilapidated place to live where we will live alone for all eternity, because we made ourselves our own god and are simply not drawn to those of opposite character, but repelled? Or will it be a large and unimaginably beautiful house in which the Lord dwells with us for all eternity? So many people today are making the most immoral choices, oblivious to what they are doing to their very own moral identity (character) and the possibility of achieving their destiny (threatening it), all for the sake of temporary goods, pleasures that will not last because our life here does not last. Whatever moral character we bring with us into eternity, that's what we live with forever, and that character determines who and what we will be attracted to. That is precisely why those who go through life with a conflict of conscience, who are unrepentant of a sin committed at one time, are simply not drawn to the Mass and the practice of the faith. That only continues in eternity. And so the time of choosing and shaping that dwelling place is now, and if we can't stand to look at ourselves in the mirror of eternity, we will be miserable forever.

The way to beautiful character is to become the person that God intends us to become. If we make choices in accordance with his will, if we are faithful to His commandments—all of them, not most of them—, if we conform our life to Christ, we will become the beautiful dwelling places we were meant to become.

And beautiful moral character is really the secret to looking beautiful. By virtue of the unity between spirit and matter, the beauty and goodness of a soul manifests in the face. No matter how pretty a person is, if one has deficient character, if one is morally ugly, it will soon begin to appear in the face, especially in the eyes. There is a difference between a good face and a pretty face, a good face and a handsome face. You might not be very good looking by nature, i.e., no modelling agency will come knocking at your door, but you can have a good face; and you can have a pretty or handsome face, but at the same time a bad face. That's what I enjoyed most about parent/teacher interviews as a teacher; there were always at least a few parents whose faces radiate morally beautiful character—quite often a Hindu or Muslim parent. It's hard for young students to understand this, for they tend to think that a good face means a pretty face, but it does not. You can be rather ugly by nature, but have a face that radiates a tremendously beautiful moral identity. Women have also said that they have dated men who were hot and handsome, but as they got to know their character (i.e., vain, self-centered, superficial, etc.), they became less and less attractive. And the opposite is true; you can date someone who is not extraordinarily good looking, but if they have morally beautiful character, they will become increasingly attractive. Virtue, holiness, moral nobility, is the secret to looking beautiful.

The more we become conformed to Christ, the more we pray and allow him to shape our character into the person he wants us to be individually and uniquely, the happier we will become, the more beautiful we will become, and the more we will be able to live with ourselves. We can't live with ourselves if Christ is not living with us. Without him, we very subtly begin to despise ourselves, but with him, we see ourselves and others as he sees us, and life becomes far more beautiful.

2. You Are What You Will

In Scripture, the heart refers to the will. Christ exhorts us to pay attention to what the heart is focused on. He said: "Where your treasure is, there your heart will be also." The heart describes what we love with our entire self. St. Theresa of Lisieux always said that you are what you will; you are what you love. You are not what you think, and you are not what you feel; but you are what you will, that is, what you ultimately love.

I remember telling that to a mental health patient whom I visited years ago; he struggled all his life with a mental illness. I had no idea the notion that 'you are what you will' would make such an impact on him. It is a crucial point for moral philosophy and theology, because we determine our moral identity, our character, by the moral choices that we make, and so you are what you choose because you will what you choose.

This was extraordinarily good news to him that you are not what you think, and you are not what you feel. If you can't help but think that you are nothing, that you are deficient, not even fully human, unlovable, perhaps because of circumstances in the past (perhaps you had a father who just would not love you or affirm you in any way and you just cannot get it out of your mind that you are unlovable and good for nothing), well some patients find great consolation in knowing that you are not necessarily what you think you are—especially if you suffer from psychotic episodes at times and really think you are something else entirely.

And if you feel deficient, if you feel like you are absolutely nothing, worthless, that you are the slime of the earth, for example, that is certainly a difficult thing to live with and some people can't seem to change that, but you can be assured that you are not necessarily what you feel. But you are what you will, and what you will to be is, through God's grace, within our power. What matters in the end and what determines who we are ultimately is the heart, what we ultimately want—what we ultimately love. The converse is also true: I might think I am wonderful and feel great about myself, but I am not what I think and I am not what I feel. I am what I love, and some of the most devious human beings think very highly of and feel very good about themselves. What they ultimately love, however, is themselves.

This first gospel reading of Advent (Lk 21, 25-28, 34-36) focuses our attention on the heart: "Be on guard so that your hearts are not weighed down with dissipation and drunkenness". This season is a microcosmic reflection of our life. Our entire life is really an Advent, a preparation for the coming of Christ, his Second Coming, and so this life is about the formation of character, our moral identity, that is, it is about the formation of the heart. Those for whom life is not an Advent, not a preparation for eternity, couldn't care less about their character or moral identity, which is why feeling good, not beautiful character, is the motivating principle of their actions.

The interesting thing about the liturgical year is that it repeats itself; every year, we relive the liturgical year. It reminds me of that movie Groundhog Day, a comedy produced in the early 90s starring Bill Murray and Andie MacDowell. Murray plays the part of Phil Connors, who is an arrogant weatherman. His assignment is to cover the annual Groundhog Day event in Punxsutawney, Pennsylvania, but he finds himself caught in a time loop, and he is forced to relive the same day, day after day. Every morning he wakes up to the same song on the radio, and every morning the radio announces that it is Groundhog Day. He alone is aware that he's lived this day before, and he will continue to live that same day repeatedly. It takes him quite a while to realize what the meaning of this time loop is, but before he learns its meaning, he tries everything, from a life of total hedonism to suicide. His suicide attempt doesn't work; he still finds himself in bed the next morning, forced to re-live that day. But eventually he begins to reflect upon his life and what is really important, and when he finally lives out the day as he ought to, that is, when he finally discovers that life has something to do with loving others for their sake, not for his own sake, he is ready to move on, and he is released from the time loop. He is overjoyed when he wakes up the following morning to a different song and a new day.

The liturgical year can be looked upon as a kind of time loop. We're called to live and relive that liturgical year, to walk with Christ and in Christ, to accompany him every year at his birth in order to learn what it means to be a child again—since he calls us to change and become as little children. And we accompany him every year on the road to Calvary, in order to really learn the meaning of human suffering and human love. And it takes a lifetime to learn how to live that liturgical year as we ought to live it. But hopefully we get better every year. That happens when we carefully reflect on where we go wrong and what needs to be done differently.

The first message of the year is that this life will come to an end, and that this life is about preparing for a Second Coming. And we are warned: the end will come for all of us, and so beware that your hearts do not become drowsy. When we are drowsy, we begin to fall asleep, and when we sleep, we take a posture identical to that which is ours when we are dead. Sleep is a metaphor for spiritual death. Jesus is exhorting us to stay awake, to stay alive, and it is divine grace that is the principle that makes us spiritually alive, and it is the decision to give ourselves over to sin that kills the grace of God within the soul; and the result is we die spiritually. The image of the life of sin in this gospel is "Carousing and drunkenness and disordered anxiety about our life". It is the life that makes the self the center around which my life revolves. This life is about learning to place Christ at the center. That takes a lifetime, because sin is easy, virtue is difficult.

But every year is to be a renewed effort to repent of choices that are inconsistent with a life in the Person of Christ, and a renewed effort to make those choices that Christ demands of us. The rich man asked Jesus what must I do to enter into eternal life, and he said: you know the commandments: you shall not steal, you shall not commit adultery, you shall not kill, honor your father and mother, etc. He said this because heaven isn't a club med vacation that we will be rewarded with if we keep the commandments. Rather, our choices determine our moral identity, and in heaven, we will wear our identity like clothing. In this world, our clothing conceals us, in heaven, our clothing reveals our deepest moral identity, who we are. It will be either beautiful clothing that reveals a beautiful moral identity, or it will be not so beautiful clothing, in which case we will flee from the gaze of God and the communion of saints in shame. This life is short, we're just passing through. Let us pray that when persecution becomes more vehement—which it might before we are finished here—, that the Lord gives us the grace of courage to endure whatever we need to endure for love of him.

3. You Know the Commandments

In the first part of today's gospel (Mt 10, 19-21), a man runs up to Jesus and asks him what it is he must do to inherit eternal life. If we really think about this, Jesus' reply should surprise us. He did not say: "Love is what you must do to inherit eternal life", or words to that effect. Rather, Jesus said something far more specific. He then proceeds to list five "thou shalt nots" – call these 'negative commandments' –, and he ends off with one positive commandment: "Honor your father and your mother".

Perhaps you followed the coverage of Pope Francis on his visit to the United States; if so, you will have noticed the narrative under construction by the media, a construction begun almost immediately after he was elected to office. The narrative suggests Pope Francis has liberalized the Church and that he broke ranks with the two previous popes, and that his emphasis on the social aspects of Catholic teaching means that the other more personal aspects of Catholic teaching no longer hold. The mainstream media is desperate for a certain kind of pope and they are determined to construct one in their own image and likeness, and " The People's Pope" is that construct. That is why it is very important to read Pope Francis first hand and frequently, and not through the eyes of some other news media.

Pope Francis knows this gospel. He has read it hundreds of times. When he says the family is beautiful, the family is an image of God, and that we are called to love, etc., he knows that there are all sorts of choices that are inconsistent with love. If I were to give you instructions on how to make your way to Los Angeles by car, those instruction will inevitably include a list of negatives along with the positives. In other words, where you are headed is just as much defined by "where not to go" (what exits not to take) as it is by "where to go"; i.e., take this Interstate south and that Interstate southwest, but do not take the first exit, and do not go east on that highway, but west for 4 hours, etc. I could keep my instructions simple and tell you that if you want to go to L.A, drive south west, but in that case you probably won't get there and will likely end up in New Orleans, etc.

When Pope Francis says "Love" and some people, many of whom haven't seen the inside of a Church in years, begin to cheer and commentators smile with great delight, you have to wonder whether or not this excitement is a manifestation of a serious case of self-deception. We live in a broken world; fetal body parts are for sale, men are leaving their wives and children for the younger looking woman at the office, countless men are addicted to Internet pornography, people are selling their souls for financial security, but so many are smitten by Pope Francis' message of love. Many of them are smitten because they really believe that because he speaks generally and does not get down to specifics that the specifics don't matter. As long as we love, everything is okay. Whatever choices we make, as long as we love the poor and the disenfranchised, we are in good standing, and who is anyone to judge us?

But this is a caricature. This is not the Holy Father. He is a son of the Church, as he has said before, and he is a follower of Christ, and when Christ was asked what must I do to enter eternal life, he said: "You know the commandments: You shall not kill; you shall not commit adultery; you shall not steal; you shall not bear false witness; you shall not defraud; honor your father and your mother" (Mk 10, 19-21). It's almost as if Jesus is suggesting the man is deceiving himself: Why are you asking me? You know the answer. Killing another human being, either physically or his very reputation, is inconsistent with love, both love of God and love of neighbor, for God brought that life into being out of love; committing adultery is a crime against marriage and marriage is holy, a sign of the love that Christ has for his Bride (the Church) and thus it tarnishes that reflection and hurts children, leaving them with scars that they will carry for the rest of their lives, not to mention the spouse that was cheated on; theft is inconsistent with love of God and neighbor, it is a failure to respect a person's fundamental right to property; lying and fraud are inconsistent with love of God and neighbor and the repercussions reach far beyond anything we can imagine – they destroy trust, and the result is we feel we live in a world in which no one can be trusted, and such an atmosphere begets other destructive behaviors, like substance abuse, despair, and even suicide. And failing to honor your father and mother – harboring unforgiveness against them throughout our lives, choosing only to look at them from our own point of view – is inconsistent with love of God and neighbor. Jesus could have gone on, but the man got the picture.

Many have convinced themselves that killing an unborn child or deliberately killing a terminally ill cancer patient by an overdose is consistent with the love of God and neighbor, that selling pornography and cheating on your income tax and pilfering things from the office and lying under oath are consistent with love of God, and that the only thing God demands is that we have compassion on a general level and vote a certain way. This is self-deception.

But Jesus goes further, because the man insists that he has observed all these commandments from his youth. Jesus sees right into his heart: there is one thing left for you to do, he says. Jesus knows he has not given his life over to God. His life does not belong to God; this man still belongs to himself, he is still the master of his own life. He does not trust in divine providence. So Jesus tells him to surrender that control over to God: Go, sell what you have, and give to the poor and you will have treasure in heaven; then come, follow me.

To follow Jesus involves much more than believing certain propositions, it means allowing Jesus to lead. If the rich man sells everything he has, he will learn soon enough that God will take care of him. That's why Jesus instructed his Apostles, when he sent them out in pairs, to take nothing for the journey except a staff – no bread, no bag, no money; he wanted them to experience their own radical dependency and the care of divine providence, that it is real, that God really is in control, that God does look after their needs. So many people do not know this because they refuse to risk it. They don't trust that God will look after them and that God orders everything providentially so that "all things work for good for those who love God" (Rm 8, 28). And so they don't know that joy and security of living in a world in which God is governor and ruler; all they know is the insecurity of living in a world in which so many look out for themselves only and will kill, cheat, lie and steal if they feel that doing so will bring them more happiness. And that is the root of so much of our behaviour that is sinful: a lack of trust in divine providence.

Be wary of the false narrative that depicts our Holy Father as some sort of Marxist who thinks personal morality does not matter. The Holy Spirit has given us a pope who is as son of the Church and a disciple of Christ.

4. The Beatitudes: The Basic Contours of a Life in Christ

*I shall pour clean water over you and you will be cleansed...
I shall give you a new heart, and put a new spirit in you; I shall
remove the heart of stone from your bodies and give you a heart of
flesh instead. I shall put my spirit in you, and make you keep
my laws and sincerely respect my observances. You will live in the
land which I gave your ancestors. You shall be my people and I
will be your God" (Ez 36, 26).*

Christians believe that God fulfilled this promise in the
Person of Christ who gathers from every nations (*kata holos*)
all who belong to God, and he forms them into the new
Israel through a new covenant. The beatitudes are the basic
outline, the interior contours, of this new spirit. Jesus, the
new Moses, writes these not on tablets of stone, but on the
human heart transformed and elevated by grace. Thus, the
new law is an interior law.

The Greek philosopher Aristotle pointed out that
genuine happiness (*eudaemonia*) is complete, enduring, and
sufficient unto itself. This means that it is not dependent
upon outside factors like the weather or the stock market.
That is why true happiness endures and is stable. But
happiness was not possible for everyone, according to
Aristotle, and the happiness of which he speaks is natural
happiness, the result of emotional stability brought about
by the virtues and the joy of natural contemplation of the
highest things. Jesus, on the other hand, is God in the flesh,
and God became man so that man could "become" God,
so to speak, that is, so that he might be "divinized", or
elevated by divine grace, which is a sharing in the
supernatural life of God. It is by entering into the Person of
Christ that we enter into his joy.

Each beatitude begins with *Makarios* ("Blessed are..."), which refers to a blessedness that is sufficient unto itself, complete, and the first taste of life eternal. The Beatitudes are everything that Aristotle was looking for, but he could not find the "formula". The reason is that the formula is a Person, one who cannot be discovered by means of human reason. He must reveal himself to us in a way that conforms to our natural mode of knowing, which is "through sense perception". The Beatitudes describe the spirit of the one who lives in the Person of Christ; they are the fundamental contours of the new life that Christ came to draw us into.

"Blessed are the Poor in Spirit; the kingdom of heaven is theirs."

Poverty of Spirit is the first and most fundamental condition for belonging to Christ, and thus the first condition for entering into the joy of the kingdom of God. Those who are poor in terms of material wealth are deeply aware of their lack. Similarly, those who are poor in spirit are aware of their spiritual lack, their fundamental inadequacies, and their radical need for God. It is only on condition of such an awareness that they will choose to open themselves up to Him. The result of that simple act of openness is the gift of the kingdom of heaven.

Mental illness is a very painful condition to have to deal with, but what I have found over the years is that many of those who suffer from mental illness have an acute awareness of their utter need for God, their poverty of spirit, and this has led them to call out to God in the midst of their darkness, which in turn has led to very intense moments of prayer. These are people selected by Christ to keep him company in Gethsemane where he experienced a heavy weight of mental anguish. Mental illness is a difficult cross, but it is a gift in many ways. Indeed, it is a painful gift, but if we consider those who live in prosperity, who are rarely sick and are so well off that their days are spent fulfilling their every whim, we notice that many of them have no awareness of their need for God and so they do not pray, and because of that they do not know *makarios*, that self-sufficient and enduring blessedness that will evolve and eventually unfold into the unimaginable joy of eternal life.

"Blessed are those who mourn, for they shall be comforted."

It seems rather counterintuitive that the mournful can be called 'happy', but this beatitude refers to a special kind of mourning. If we love God, we will love all those who belong to God, and every human being without exception comes from God and is loved by God with an incomprehensible love. And so the more we enter into the heart of God, the more we discover our neighbor there, and so we are moved to return to earth, so to speak, and we go looking for him or her, because we know that there we will find the God we have begun to love: we discover our neighbor in God, and we rediscover God in our neighbor.

Now when we truly love others, their happiness becomes our own, because we have begun to love them as "another self", and yet for the most part, we find them in pain, suffering, and struggling to be happy. Because we love them as "another self", their suffering too becomes our own. We mourn for them, for it is so hard to remain indifferent to the sufferings of others after we have discovered and entered into the heart of God. It is the sins of human beings, the cold indifference of others towards God and neighbor that fills us with sorrow. This, however, is a blessed sorrow, a sorrow that is not incompatible with joy, but exists with it, for it is the joy of having been invited into Christ's sorrow, which is a joy filled sorrow.

"Blessed are the meek, for they shall inherit the earth."

A meek spirit is a gentle spirit. The poor in spirit who mourn the misery of others because they really know that misery and are moved to share in it are gentle towards those who are suffering. The meek are not quick to take offense at others; they are very patient with others because they know that God has always been patient with them. When we take a good hard look at how often we have been wrong over the years, how often our impressions, inferences, conjectures, conclusions, convictions, etc., have turned out to be mistaken, we tend to be less self-righteous, less confident in the way we see and interpret the actions of others. We hesitate to draw definitive conclusions, and thus it becomes easier to be more patient with others, gentler, and more open to listening to them, whomever they might be. Anger is a response to an injustice, but often what we interpret as an injustice is, on closer inspection, no such thing. Those who are quick to react with anger are disposed to make rapid inferences and to trust too readily in the way they interpret things, believing that their grasp of the real is far more accurate and comprehensive than it is in reality.

But when a person finally realizes how tiny is the conceptual framework in which he sees and interprets the world at any one time, he tends to be more open to learning and is reluctant to jump to conclusions, and thus much less prone to react in anger. The meek are self-possessed, in control of their emotions, in particular the passion of anger. Meekness, however, does not mean the suppression of anger. Recall that Jesus became angry at the money changers in the temple and drove them out. Anger that is governed by reason and is a response to real injustice is not sinful, but virtuous; the deliberate decision to keep anger alive in a spirit of unforgiveness, however, is sinful.

"Blessed are those who hunger and thirst for what is right; they shall be satisfied."

Hunger and thirst, as these words are used here, are something that few of us in the western world have experienced. What Jesus is referring to is the hunger pangs of a first century Palestinian laborer who knew what it was like to go without food for an extended period of time, and the thirst is that of a Palestinian who has experienced the heat of the desert and the thirst it induces. There is a tremendous amount of indifference in this world, and the reason is that indifference is rather painless. The indifferent do not suffer over the wounds and miseries of others; many in fact secretly delight in the misfortunes of others, which is why bad news spreads quickly. Many are simply not incensed at the injustices around them, and although they are very passionate about their goals, those ambitions often have little to do with making this a more just world and more to do with their own individual fulfillment.

But an indication that the Lord is drawing you into himself, into his own life, is that you are the kind of person who loves justice more than you love yourself, as opposed to the kind of person who looks out for himself first, and only later, after all his needs are met, concerns himself with others. Those who have entered into Christ will suffer a great deal of hunger and thirst, because there is so much injustice around us. The more intense your love, the more intense your hunger and thirst; blessed are you if you live with this kind of hunger and thirst, because that means you have entered into the hunger and thirst of Christ.

"Blessed are the merciful; they will be shown mercy."

Christ revealed God as absolute mercy. He came to die for us and cancel the debt of sin, which we were unable to pay. The Latin word for mercy is *misericordia* (*miser, cor, dia*).

The word means "the heart (*cor*) of God (*deus*) touching our misery (*miser*). God enters into our misery by becoming man in the Person of Christ. He does so to inject the comfort of his presence into the depths of our darkness so that when life becomes dark for us, we do not have to suffer alone. When we have been touched by his mercy, we too become merciful; to follow him is to become a channel of his mercy.

"Blessed are the pure in heart; they shall see God."

What is pure is unmixed. For example, we speak of pure maple syrup that is unmixed with anything else. To be pure in heart is to have an undivided love for God, a heart unmixed with any other competing love. Some people love creation more than the Creator; they love things to the point of worshipping things, such as wealth, or the pleasures of the earth, the glorification of the self, etc. They may even love God, but their love is mixed with a disordered love of self. In other words, the center of their lives is, in the end, the self.

Aristotle said: "As a person is, so does he see". What we see and don't see is in large part determined by our character, the kind of person we've made ourselves to be by our moral choices. We are what we love. The 'heart' is the most important factor in determining what it is we are able to see. It is always delightful to have a discussion with a group of young grade nine students who are both highly intelligent and who still have the purity and innocence of childhood. Some of them are able to achieve a level of understanding of the loftiest theological concepts, something no longer possible for many senior students who have lost that purity. That is why the pure of heart shall see God, who calls us to love Him more than His gifts. If we eventually get to that point, we shall see Him as He is in Himself (the Beatific Vision).

"Blessed are the peacemakers; they shall be called the children of God."

The Latin word for peace is *pax*, which means unity. As Ezekiel prophesied, the Lord will gather his people together from all nations; for love unites, while hate divides. A peacemaker is one who strives to bring together, to maintain a genuine harmony among people. A peacemaker is not a "peacenik"; rather, he is one who is willing to 'make' peace, to work for it, even to fight for it. An unjust aggressor, which might include an entire nation, is intent on destroying the peace, so a true peacemaker is willing to take up arms and fight, perhaps die for the *pax* of the nation, as our war veterans have done. So there is no requirement that one become a pacifist if one is a Christian.

Gossipers are not peacemakers, but love scandal and division. Controllers too are not genuine peacemakers; indeed, the controller (i.e., a controlling pastor) desires to gather into a unity, but one that is under his control and that he can manage. He attempts to order everything for the sake of securing a safe environment for himself. If the controller is a priest or bishop, he may betray the duties of his office by refusing to speak out when necessary, by remaining silent on difficult moral matters because he loves his own "peace of mind" more than he loves the good of the flock. He may be tempted to rationalize his silence under the pretext of being a "peacemaker", that is, one who does not wish to "divide". But this is an attitude contrary to Christ: "Do not suppose I have come to bring peace to the earth: it is not peace I have come to bring, but a sword" (Mt 10, 34).

The true peacemaker, however, is not an "organizer", but an instrument in the hands of Christ who orders and "brings together" in ways that are beyond our comprehension at the moment. It is only much later, when looking back, that we see that what appeared to be a life characterized by unintelligible randomness was really an ordered movement towards the realization of the larger plan of divine providence.

"Blessed are those who are persecuted for the sake of what is right, for theirs is the kingdom of heaven."

This final beatitude clearly implies that there is a real difference between joy and pleasure; for there is no pleasure in being persecuted, but you do find a secret joy in the very recesses of the soul, for you have become aware that you've received the gift of being drawn into the very heart of his silence. Christ is joy, and it is in being persecuted on account of him that you and I really come to know him. The silence of Christ is more joyful than the greatest joys the earth has to offer, and this is what persecution on account of Christ does for us, it takes us out of the noise of the world and into the profound rest of his other worldly silence.

This beatitude clearly implies that Jesus is no mere human being. How absurd it would be for me to call anyone blessed for suffering persecution on my account. What power do I have to offer them any kind of blessedness for what they choose to undergo for me? But Jesus can impart *makarios* to those who suffer on account of belonging to him, because he is no mere man; he is fully God and fully man, and as God he chose to join a human nature to inject human suffering with the very joy of his supernatural life, which is so different from any other joy that indeed it strikes one silent. We rest in him; for we have found in him everything that the human heart is looking for but cannot find outside of him.

5. Share Your Bread

The readings of the 5th Sunday in Ordinary Time are very straightforward; they are taken from Isaiah 58, 7-10; 1 Corinthians 2, 1-5; and the gospel of Matthew, 5, 13-16. Essentially, we are to be a light in the darkness. The only way to be a light in the darkness is allow ourselves to be lit, like a candle that is brought close to the flame that it may catch fire. And of course that flame is Christ, who is the light of the world. There is only one light of the world, and Christ is it, and so if we are to be a light in the darkness, we can only do so by drawing close to him, so close as to catch fire.

The first reading from Isaiah says: "Share your bread with the hungry, shelter the oppressed and the homeless, clothe the naked when you see them, and to not turn your back on them". Of course, this is precisely how we are going to be judged, according to the parable of the Last Judgment: "I was hungry and you gave me something to eat, thirsty and you gave me something to drink, naked and you clothed me, etc." Our love for Christ corresponds precisely to the love we have for those who are least among us. As St. John of the Cross said "In the evening of life, we will be judged on love alone", that is, on how we have loved those who need to be loved, who have not known love throughout their lives.

I know of a man who is quite well off; he owns a multi-million dollar home in a very wealthy neighborhood, not to mention a cottage of about the same price. His is a life of travel, cruises, scuba diving, dining in the finest restaurants, etc. And he will often remark: "I wonder what the poor people are doing today?" expressed not in a tone of deep consternation for them, but in a condescending one that delights in his prosperity and supposed superiority over the less fortunate. That is a man who does not know how fragile his life is; for in no time at all, he could very well end up on the street, or in a nursing home completely dependent upon the care of others. If he really wanted to know how the poor are doing, he could enter into their lives and devote himself to relieving their suffering, at least to some limited extent. But his life is all about indulging in the pleasures that his wealth can buy. Although this man enjoys tremendous leisure, he lives in darkness; a poor person who has little but who has the faith to make his way to Mass regularly and the faith to delight in that Mass is much richer.

Consider what the first reading said about that person who shares his bread with the hungry and shelters the oppressed and homeless: "Then your light shall break forth like the dawn, and your wound shall quickly be healed." That's an interesting line. There are so many people in this world carrying around a huge weight of painful memories and hurts buried in their subconscious. The way to healing is to serve those in need, to put the suffering before oneself; for when we are sick, all we can think of is ourselves. If you have a fever, all you can think of is how uncomfortable you are; it's very difficult to think of others. And that's why we are living in such a cold world that is indifferent to the sufferings of others; because people are carrying around in themselves a reservoir of emotional wounds that they are barely conscious of. But, share your bread with the hungry, clothe the naked when you see them, and do not turn your back on your own, and your wound shall be quickly healed. The reason is that we are drawing close to Christ, who dwells in the hearts of the suffering. He lives in their suffering, because he joined them in their suffering when he joined a human nature to himself and dwelt among us. And just as your clothes will catch fire if you draw to close to the fire, so too, draw close to him in the persons of those who suffer and you will catch that living flame of his love. Then you will be healed.

Your eyes will no longer be focused on yourself, on your own pain, because you will be healed.

Most people believe that if I am to be happy, I have to fill myself up with experiences. But these readings say the opposite. If I am to be happy, I have to pour myself out, forget about my own experiences and instead focus my attention on the experiences of others, that is, be attuned to their suffering. Then a joy and light enters the soul, and we become a light in the darkness. The interior of our own life is filled with light, and that light also radiates outward, making life a bit brighter for others.

Catholicism is not about having the right answers, as many young and energetic Catholics seem to believe it is; rather, Catholicism is about Christ. It's about knowing him and knowing his cross, knowing (via union) the love that appears to us from that cross. St. Paul said he came to Corinth not with persuasive words of wisdom, or eloquent arguments; he came in weakness and fear and much trembling, in other words, he came in the power of the cross, so that their faith would rest not on argument or human wisdom, but on the power of God. The cross alone conquered death. No human power could conquer death. Only the cross. And that's our power; it has been given to us to use. We just have to pray in a spirit of trust, fully aware that we cannot accomplish anything on our own, but we can do all things in him (Phil 4, 13). In the complete awareness of our limitations, all we have to do is rely on him, to live our lives in him, to pray in him, and we will accomplish what no human person with great power and intelligence and influence can do outside of him.

6. Detach Yourself and Give Alms

More than twenty times throughout the New
Testament Jesus tells us not to be afraid. And there really is
nothing for us to fear, because everything is subject to the
providence of God; nothing happens to us without His
permission, and whatever He permits to happen to us who
belong to Him, He permits ultimately for our greatest good;
for He desires our greatest good and has the power to bring
it about. As Jesus said here, "Your Father is pleased to give
you the kingdom".

This world is not the kingdom, no matter how
wonderful our life is here; for the kingdom of God does
not pass away, it is eternal. But just as the sun is too bright
for us to gaze at for any extended length of time, so too the
kingdom of God exceeds the capacity of our soul. We have
to be prepared or properly disposed for the kingdom of
God, and we do this by detaching from a disordered love of
this world and directing ourselves towards the kingdom of
God, which is God Himself, God who is Love. Our soul
has to be gradually detached from the love of self and more
deeply attached to the love of God.

But God dwells among us; He hides Himself under a
very real disguise, and He told us where we can find Him.
He said in the parable of the Last Judgment: "I was hungry,
and you gave me something to eat, thirsty, and you gave me
something to drink, sick and you visited me...as long as you
did this for the least of my brethren, you did it for me" (Mt
25, 31-46). That is why immediately after urging us not to
be afraid, Jesus said: "Sell your belongings and give alms."
That's the detachment: "Sell your belongings", get rid of
what you do not need, all that is weighing you down and
binding you to this world. At the end of the summer we
often see colourful hot air balloons in the sky over North
York. It must be exhilarating to ride in one of those
balloons. But there is no rising from the earth unless the

line that secures the balloon to the earth is completely detached from the ground. So too with us, there is no rising towards God until we begin to detach from the love of this world.

But detachment is not enough, even for the balloon. It needs hot air to rise, and that comes from the flame. So too, we need the flame of the divine love to raise us to God. That is why in this gospel, Jesus immediately said: "Give alms". With the excess money that we get from selling all that weighs us down and keeps us attached to the earth, give alms, turn towards the poor and the needy, think of them, serve them, because they are a tabernacle in which Christ dwells. He said it himself: "…as long as you did this for the least of my brethren, you did it for me".

Giving alms is an act of love. If we begin to love God in loving and serving the poor, we will come to know him intimately. We will know him not just from the outside, from hearing about him, but from within, by actually loving him in the poor. We never really know anyone just by reading about them, but only by loving them do we come to know them.

At the end of this gospel, Christ speaks of punishment. That servant who knew his master's will but did not make preparations nor act in accord with his will shall be "beaten severely" (Lk 12, 47). That's a pretty serious warning. The person who does not use this life to prepare for heaven, but lives his life for himself, whose treasure is here in this world, such a person will enter eternity with a soul completely indisposed to delight in the joy of heaven—which is God and the communion of His saints. To exist forever, in eternity, with a heart that was created for God, for the possession of God, but forever deprived of that possession, is hell. It is very difficult to imagine the pain of hell, but there are ways of coming to some appreciation of it. There is an episode of *The Twighlight Zone* called "A Nice Place to Visit". The story is about a crook named Rocky

Valentine. It starts off that he's in the middle of a robbery, and soon the sirens are going. He ends up getting shot by a police officer as he was making his escape down an alley. He wakes up, and there standing next to him is a man in a white suit who looks like Burl Ives, whose name is Pip. He is Rocky Valentine's guide in this new after life of his.

Rocky is given everything he desires, i.e., money, nice clothes that fit perfectly, three beautiful women, a beautiful penthouse apartment, the finest cigars, and he loves to gamble. At the casino he is winning all the time, no matter what game he plays, whether it's roulette or a slot machine; the money continues to pour in. Every day he feasts on the finest foods; when he plays a game of pool, he hits a perfect shot every time. None of this changes his heart, however. He still feels resentment when a tall police officer walks by, and since his wish is that the officer be humiliated in some way, his wish is granted—the officer is reduced in size to a small boy. At one point he tries to recall what good deed he ever did in his life that made up for all the bad he's ever done; in his mind, that would explain why he's enjoying this heavenly bliss. To answer this question, his guide Pip takes him to the Hall of Records. He reads his file, but all he reads are his past crimes. He can't find a good deed in his record, so he shrugs his shoulders and goes off to fool around with his girls and to gamble a bit more; his guide tells him if he needs anything to just call him by dialling PIP.

He's back in the Casino, still winning, but he just doesn't care anymore. In the next scene he's surrounded by his three girls playing poker in bed, and of course he wins with a royal flush, the ladies having nothing but admiration for him. But he's fed up and kicks them out of his room, insulting them on their way out. He's terribly frustrated, so he picks up the phone and dials for Pip. When his guide appears, he tells him that he's been here a month and he can't stand it anymore. "I'm bored, I'm bored," he says.

Well, his guide gives him the option of returning to his former way of life. If he wants, he can rob a bank or a convenience store, and he will even arrange for a get-away car of his choice. In desperation, Rocky asks: "Is there a chance that I could get caught?" Pip replies: "Of course, I'll just make a note of it". Whatever Rocky wants, he gets.

But Rocky sees this is pointless. "There's no meaning", he says. And so Rocky tells Pip: "I just don't think I belong here, I just don't fit in". He says "If I have to stay here another day, I'm gonna go nuts. Look, I don't belong in heaven. I want to go to the other place". Pip replies: "Heaven? Whatever gave you the idea you're in heaven, Mr. Valentine? This is the other place". Rocky's face is struck with horror, and he tries to open the doors, but he cannot. It ends with the narrator: "A scared angry little man who never got a break, now he has everything he's ever wanted, and he's going to have to live with it for eternity".

It's a brilliant image of hell—the eternal love of self, forever trapped in the small world one has made for oneself.

But now imagine what it would be like to be forever in the presence of those who have loved only themselves, who love sin more than they love God, those whose love for human beings was always a matter of self-love: they loved others only for what they could do for them. Outside of that, they had no use for others. To have to exist forever in the realm of the damned is unthinkable. The basic food of the soul is love, for we were created to love and be loved— to love God above all things, and to be loved by God, who loves each one of us as if there is only one of us. To have rejected that in favour of prosperity in this temporary world is unthinkable stupidity.

Many people die without having prepared for eternal life with God. As a chaplain who spent many years with the dying once said to me: "Generally speaking, people die as they live. If they live without God, they typically die without God". If they live never having developed a prayer life, an interior life, they die without an interior life. If they have lived loving only themselves, they die loving only themselves. The eternal existence that they have freely determined for themselves is nothing other than hell.

But our preparation begins here by trusting in God, listening to Christ when he tells us not to be afraid, by detaching ourselves from all the riches that we possess out of a fear that we will be left without, and by thinking of the poor and giving alms regularly. The angel Raphael, in the book of Tobit, says: "Prayer with fasting and alms with right conduct are better than riches with iniquity. Better to practise almsgiving than to hoard up gold. Almsgiving saves from death and purges every kind of sin. Those who give alms have their fill of days; those who commit sin and do evil, bring harm on themselves" (Tb 12, 8-10).

7. Called from the Womb

Pay attention, you people from far away! The Lord called me before I was born, while I was in my mother's womb he named me (Is 49, 1-2).

Recently I heard a prayer that was said in public, and there was a line that said: "Lord, help me to fulfill all my dreams…" I asked my young students to think about the prayer and consider whether or not something in it was amiss. They didn't think so, probably because that's their prayer, that the Lord would help them to fulfill all their dreams. I remember well my teenage years; I was full of dreams. They made my young life exhilarating; and I resented it when some adult would try to snap me out of my semi-delusional existence and into reality.

But the fact of the matter is that God does not help us to fulfill our dreams. Rather, He calls us to help Him fulfill His providential plan. A very important stage in personality development, in fact, is called "the End of the Dream". Dreams are exciting, and they an essential part of being young, but the Lord has a vocation for us. He called us before we were born, and while we were in our mother's womb He named us. For the Jews, to be named is to be given one's identity, one's specific purpose in life. We should never pray that the Lord help us fulfill our dreams, but rather that our dreams coincide with His will, that we come to want what He wants for us.

The Lord has given each one of us gifts, both natural and supernatural, and He gave us these gifts for a reason, and it was not so that we could fulfill our dreams; those gifts were given us in view of our own unique vocation, our own unique place that God has for us in this world. He wants to place us, and if I cooperate and allow Him to place me, if I pray and stay close to God in order to eventually hear that call and discern where it is He wills to place me so that I may serve His will, if I discover that, I will have found my greatest happiness. Our greatest happiness (our deepest desire) is found in taking our limited place assigned by God and serving Him with all our mind, our heart, and strength.

There is so much unhappiness in this world, so much discontent, because so many people have missed their vocation, and they missed it because they thought their lives were about fulfilling their dreams, and many of these people have fulfilled their dreams, but they have discovered that they are no happier than when they started out. They never bothered to pray and ask God to show them the way. Instead, they expected that God would be their servant.

But, as Isaiah says in this first reading: "And now the Lord says, who formed me in the womb to be his servant, to bring Jacob back to him, and that Israel might be gathered to him, for I am honoured in the sight of the Lord, and my God has become my strength" (Is 49, 5).

We are His servants, and it is our greatest honour to be such a thing. This world is His, not ours, and our life is His, not ours. But many people will try to usurp what belongs to God, and so they claim this world as their own, and they believe their lives are their own, to do with as they wish, even destroy it.

We've witnessed tremendous crimes against human life in the 20th century, and we've seen a steady devaluation of human life since World War II. Truman attempted to justify his decision to drop the a-bomb on Hiroshima through a utilitarian ethics. In his letters, he explicitly refers to this act as murderous, but he justifies it on the basis of the principle that it is permissible to do evil to achieve good, a principle that was explicitly repudiated by St. Paul (Rom 3, 8). Many scholars argue that this murderous act of intentionally destroying innocent non-combatants, carried out to demoralize the Japanese army, was just the beginning, that this opened the door to the eventual rationalization of other anti-life choices, most notably the deliberate destruction of developing human life in the womb. But, as the psalm says: "I praise you, for I am wonderfully made; for it was you who formed my inward parts; you knit me together in my mother's womb....My frame was not hidden from you, when I was being made in secret, intricately woven in the depths of the earth..." (139, 13-16).

In that light, it is very clear that abortion is not simply the destruction of a developing human life, it is the destruction of a vocation, a unique and unrepeatable call; it is the willful opposition to a divine summons addressed to the unborn child.

Although we believe this, we must keep in mind that it is not for us to judge the heart of any individual human being. I know all sorts of women who have had an abortion that they regret, and a number of these women are some of the most powerful witnesses to the culture of life today. As former abortionist Bernard Nathanson reminds us, we need to keep in mind that we don't live in a culture of life anymore and that many people have been kept in the dark about the nature of human life in the womb; hence, the unborn child is not the only victim, women themselves are victims; they have not been told the truth of what takes place in the womb during such a procedure. So it is important to keep our eyes on the issue and renounce all inclination to judge the heart of another human being— there is so much we just don't know when it comes to the circumstances and conditions of individual persons, so we best leave judgment to God.

But there is no doubt that we simply cannot imagine how different this world would be right now had we chosen, as a country, as a culture, to revere human life, especially at its most helpless and vulnerable stage of development. And now, as so many predicted, this anti-life mentality that refuses to recognize that God is the Lord of life, not us, this mentality has finally opened the door in Canada to active euthanasia, or what others like to refer to as doctor assisted suicide.

Part of our vocation is to witness to the sanctity of human life, to bring people back to Him, that this country might be gathered to Him. We're going to win this battle for the culture of life only if we respond with great charity and a willingness to witness visibly, all the while refusing to make judgments on the guilt of others—as I said, some of the most influential witnesses in favor of life are women who have had abortions, not to mention former abortionists. If we open up channels of communication and dialogue in a spirit that reveres and respects those who oppose us, we'll move forward towards that culture of life that Pope John Paul II prayed so much for. And the way towards this is not to point fingers, but to continue to call attention to the baby in the womb, who has a beating heart, a brain, hands and feet, fingers and toes, and an instinct to fight for its life. John the Baptist leapt for joy in the womb of his mother when he heard Mary greeting her at the Visitation. Let us pray to St. John the Baptist to intercede for us and for our leaders that a culture of life may be re-established.

8. The Cost of Grace

One cannot read the Acts of the Apostles without coming to some awareness that there is a cost of discipleship. The world, however, prefers a discipleship at very low cost, including grace. In his classic work, *The Cost of Discipleship*, Dietrich Bonhoeffer writes, 'Cheap grace is the preaching of forgiveness without requiring repentance, (it is) baptism without Church discipline, communion without confession, absolution without personal confession. Cheap grace is grace without discipleship, grace without the cross, grace without Jesus Christ, living and incarnate." (The Cost of Discipleship, p. 36. SCM Press Ltd. London, 1976)

The world prefers everything cheap, at the lowest cost possible. For some things, such as food, clothing, and housing, etc., this is reasonable; resources are scarce. For other things, however, we best keep in mind that "you get what you pay for", as the saying goes. Information about who Pope Francis is and what he stands for is being purchased at a very low cost, and if your information about who he is cost you little in terms of labor, that is, the time and effort it takes to read a few headlines or take in some hearsay evidence, etc., then you got what you paid for, which was some cheap and highly unreliable information. What I have found lately is that those who typically make reference to Pope Francis in support of their ideas on the new direction the Church ought to be taking have not actually read directly from the Pope's writings, just as so many of those who back in the 80s and 90s made reference to Vatican II against the papacies of John Paul II and Pope Benedict XVI had not actually read the documents of Vatican II at all, but relied instead on headlines and popular misconceptions. This is the shortcut route to "knowledge" that many people opt for—only what we're left with is not knowledge at all.

Generally speaking, we are lazy, intellectually above all. Thinking slowly and carefully requires effort, while quick inferences on the basis of very little evidence and first impressions are much easier and more common. Students today have their iPhones and other electronic devices, and that should make life easier still, freeing up scarce resources (i.e., time) for the more important things, such as time devoted to a genuine education. Whereas before we had to wait weeks to get our hands on a book we'd ordered and paid for, now within minutes students can download great classics for free; books by Charles Dickens, Oscar Wilde, Charlotte Bronte, even Aquinas' *Summa Theologica* and *The Confessions* of St. Augustine, and much more. In addition, they can have some of the best articles written by the best political pundits in North America tweeted to them every morning. But it doesn't matter, because typically they won't read them; it is far too taxing to read a 1,500 word article, let alone *The Confessions* or sections of *The Summa*.

We tend to want everything cheap, without a great deal of effort. For example, there is and always will be only one way to lose weight, which is diet and exercise. But there's always someone trying to sell us a diet that promises weight loss without difficulty, that is, without having to give up the foods we love. Similarly, education fads are often about the false promise of purchasing an education more cheaply, that is, without the effort that a real education demands. Although students have electronic devices that are fast and efficient, there's only one way to become educated, one way to become a genuinely critical thinker, and only one way to become a person who can offer meaningful solutions to complex problems, and that is years of studying, especially a particular area of thought, and those years will involve reading and more reading, writing and more writing, thinking, discussing, opposition, self-correcting, learning from the great masters of the past, as well as more contemporary thinkers. Any school or new educational messiah that promises educators a revolutionary technique that will accomplish what no educator has been able to accomplish without tremendous effort—and which centuries of the best and brightest educators in the past somehow missed—, or promises young students the possibility of a good education without the hard labor that was required by those who went before us, is selling us snake oil.

If we read *The Nicomachean Ethics* of Aristotle, a classic which has been foundational for many psychologists and psychiatrists in recent years, we see that *eudaemonia,* which is the good life (or happiness), is difficult to achieve. It is difficult because it is a matter of cultivating habits; virtues are habits that dispose the passions to obey reason, and the emotions have an innate need to be guided by reason. But we all know that good habits are hard to acquire and bad habits are hard to break. That's why happiness is difficult and few ever achieve it. And that's the point, it is an achievement, a moral achievement, and not something one stumbles upon or discovers. It is an activity, not a passivity (i.e., not something received).

But the New Age and the latest self-help books have always promised happiness and well-being without the need for moral reform, without the difficult effort involved in changing our ways, renouncing evil, making sacrifices, restraining passions and impulses, etc. And that's why these authors continue to make money: that is precisely what many people want to hear and believe, and they choose to believe it despite the overwhelming evidence to the contrary.

And the same is found in the Church. Although Christ says: "Anyone who wishes to be a follower of mine, let him take up his cross and follow me", many are willing to follow as long as that cross is made of light material. For many people today, Ten Invitations is much more inviting than Ten Commandments, and we love those priests who preach cheap grace and despise those who remind us of the cost. A priest friend of mine recently visited a former SS officer in his 90s. He was a low ranking officer, and so he was not charged with crimes against humanity. However, he did cooperate with the Nazis, because he loved his life more than he loved those whom the Nazis sought to exterminate. Two things struck me about what he said to my friend. First, he pointed out that many SS officers refused to cooperate with Hitler, once they discovered what the Nazis were up to; they refused to go along, and these soldiers were taken away and killed for their decision. He emphasized that history is silent about that fact; there are no records of these heroes. The second thing that struck me is that the prospects of purgatory were delightful to this man. He is very grateful that the mercy of God freed him of the sins that have weighed him down all these years, but he knows in his heart that this wasn't cheap, but has a cost, that he has to make up for what he has done and what he failed to do, and the thought of the justice and pain of purgatory fills him with delight.

Lovers of cheap grace need to ask themselves whether or not they are on the road to salvation; for the way to eternal life is narrow and few find it, says Jesus, and the road to perdition is broad and many take it. It is very possible to attend Mass every Sunday in order to "pray our way away from God"; indeed, there are people whose coming to Church is their way of keeping God at a distance. These people know who they are, for they recoil when the raw word of God is preached; they delight in the light and "happy" message that God demands of us nothing more than a high five and a big smile. Grace, however, is not cheap, but very costly. Deitrich Bonhoeffer continues: "Costly grace is the treasure hidden in the field; for the sake of it a man will gladly go and sell all that he has. It is the pearl of great price to buy which the merchant will sell all his goods. It is the kingly rule of Christ, for whose sake a man will pluck out the eye which causes him to stumble, it is the call of Jesus Christ at which the disciple leaves his nets and follows him. Costly grace is the gospel which must be sought again and again, the gift which must be asked for, the door at which a man must knock. Such grace is costly because it calls us to follow, and it is grace because it calls us to follow Jesus Christ. It is costly because it costs a man his life, and it is grace because it gives a man the only true life. It is costly because it condemns sin, and grace because it justifies the sinner. Above all, it is costly because it cost God the life of his Son: 'ye were bought at a price', and what has cost God much cannot be cheap for us. Above all, it is grace because God did not reckon his Son too dear a price to pay for our life, but delivered him up for us. Costly grace is the Incarnation of God." (*Ibid.*, p. 36-37)

9. Remaining Silent on Moral Matters

Recently I heard a story of a priest who speaks of the regret he now feels at the approach he took as a young Catholic pastor in a U.S. diocese. In short, he'd resolved never to challenge the congregation on their moral lives, that is, never to bring up difficult issues of personal morality, for fear that such topics might cause others to feel uncomfortable. His intention was to keep the parish atmosphere light and communal, thus excluding even the slightest mention of any issue or topic that could cause others to feel out of place.

He admits that his approach was, in the short run, successful; he filled the Church to the rafters. What he found, however, was that after a number of years, people left. The reason is that they got tired, bored, and so they sought excitement in other more interesting and challenging pursuits. He admits and regrets that he failed to challenge their moral and spiritual lives, which needed challenging, and it was this neglect and the resulting lack of moral and spiritual awareness on their part that allowed them to eventually abandon the practice of the faith.

The human heart necessarily seeks happiness; it is the ultimate end of every choice we make. And happiness has certain characteristics: it is 1) sufficient unto itself, 2) complete, and 3) enduring. That is why many of the greatest thinkers have been, somewhat, in agreement: happiness is not pleasure, nor is it honors, but rather a specific kind of achievement, a moral achievement, that is, a life of virtue. Happiness is a matter of character, not personality, and our eternal destiny is a matter of character, that is, it hinges on the kind of person we have made ourselves to be by the moral choices that we have made throughout our lives.

The human person needs to sense that he is on the road to happiness, but this cannot happen to a congregation that is fed on morally and spiritually under-nourishing food. If a person is not challenged to aspire after something higher, that is, to aspire towards greater moral integration in his own personal life, he will not feel that he is on the road to something greater. The result is that he will begin to look for that road elsewhere, without knowing precisely what it is he's looking for. That is why those Churches that have given up on a straight-forward proclamation of the gospel that includes a powerful message of personal sacrifice and fidelity to the commandments, in favor of a more socially "relevant" and morally innocuous message are now easily identifiable from the sidewalk—they have undergone expensive makeovers and are now highly sought after condominiums. But where there is real moral and spiritual growth, there is no boredom.

The decision to avoid whatever might cause people to feel uncomfortable is simply indefensible, for it is immature and irrational. Consider what any good doctor does when he has before him a patient who feels sick. He presses down on one part of the body and asks: "Does this hurt?" If not, he moves on to another part: "Does that hurt?" etc. If nothing hurts, the patient is probably well, but if the patient grimaces in pain, the doctor knows something is wrong; for that pain is a sign that the patient is not entirely well. To refuse to press down for fear that this might cause the patient to feel uncomfortable is negligence deserving of a lawsuit.

The same is true in the spiritual life. If someone becomes upset upon hearing, for example, that reading pornography is morally wrong or about any other moral matters that bear upon one's sex life, etc., that reaction is perhaps a sign that something is profoundly amiss in the life of this person and that he or she is not entirely healthy (morally and spiritually)—of course, it could also be a healthy reaction against a priest's lack of tactfulness, timing, or unhealthy preoccupation with these issues. There are

45

prudent ways to challenge a congregation, and there are imprudent ways to do so. That many pastors have been reckless, self-righteous and pastorally incompetent in the past is no reason to remain silent now, any more than medical malpractice in the past is a reason for doctors to avoid intrusive and careful examinations in the present.

That some pastors could go through their entire priesthood unable to draw such obvious conclusions is difficult to fathom. We can speculate on the possible causes—and there is no doubt in my mind that the reasons have little to do with theology and everything to do with psychology—, but whatever the reason, it is even more difficult to understand how such a person who regularly reads the breviary can fail to notice a fundamental conflict between his own pastoral approach and the theme of the readings, repeated every fall season, that bear upon the shepherd who neglects his flock for the sake of his own comfort and peace of mind: "You, son of man, I have appointed watchman for the house of Israel; when you hear me say anything, you shall warn them for me. If I tell the wicked man that he shall surely die, and you do not speak out to dissuade the wicked man from his way, he shall die for his guilt, but I will hold you responsible for his death" (Ez 33, 7-8).

10. Creating a Catholic Culture in the Home

At only 12 years of age, the teachers of the Law were astounded at Jesus' understanding and his wisdom. Where did Jesus get his understanding? The answer is that he got it from his foster father, St. Joseph. The primary duty of the father of a Jewish household was to pass down the teachings of the Torah to his children (Cf. Ex 12, 26-27; Dt 6, 7). He also got his learning from his mother, because the mother of a Jewish household has a significant role as teacher (Cf. Prv 1, 8; 6, 20). And what were they doing in Jerusalem? Like a faithful Jewish family, they were there for the feast of Passover, and the gospel tells us that they would go every year.

The important point to remember here is that Judaism is not simply one religion alongside others. If you've ever studied the religions of the world, you know that there is something radically different about Judaism. It is not a human philosophy about how to escape the cycles of reincarnation or a philosophy about how to escape from suffering. Rather, Judaism is a revealed religion in which God has taken the initiative, not man. God revealed Himself to Abraham, promised to make him the father of a great nation if he would obey and do what God commanded. And to prove that He was serious about this promise, He made a covenant with Abraham and sealed it in the blood of an animal sacrifice. Abraham's wife eventually conceived a son, Isaac, who fathered Jacob, who had 12 sons, and Israel eventually became a nation of twelve tribes. God remembered his covenant when His people were slaves in a foreign land, and He called Moses to deliver Israel from Egyptian slavery. Pharaoh's heart was stubborn, and it was only after the last plague, the death of the first born, that he finally let Israel go. Israel spent 40 years in the desert, and it was through Moses that Israel received the Law.

Judaism is about a history; it is not a philosophy. It is about a people that God chose to be his own, a firstborn son, thus an older sibling to the nations. The content of that religion is God's fidelity, in history, to His promises.

But history exists in the memories of people, and memories fade, unless we work to keep them alive. That is why the Lord commanded Israel to celebrate festivals throughout the year, feasts that commemorate God's action in history. If they remember God's action in history, they will remain grateful; if they forget, they will lose gratitude and become an irreligious people. All the requirements of the law, the rituals in all their detail, exist for the sake of keeping history alive in the memories of the Jews.

The parents' primary duty was to pass down the teachings of the Torah to their children. All else was secondary. God was first, everything else second. We see this in the Ten Commandments; the first three have to do with God, the rest have to do with our neighbor. Clearly, Mary and Joseph fulfilled what was their primary duty, and the reaction of the teachers of the law clearly shows this.

More than ever before, it seems, we are hearing of young married couples with children breaking up after only a few years, not for serious reasons, but for reasons that reveal an alarming degree of immaturity. The reasons that are increasingly given for leaving have to do with "not feeling fulfilled", "falling out of love", "loss of excitement", etc. These young people seem to think that they have a right to feel fulfilled all the time, a right to a life of non-stop exhilaration. It is as if life and love have nothing to do with sacrifice.

Dr. Scott Peck wrote the best seller *The Road Less Traveled*, and in that book is one of the best chapters ever written on the nature of falling in love—the chapter is entitled "The Illusion of Romantic Love". He says that every couple is destined to fall out of love, and one of the worst mistakes a couple can make is to think that Romantic love, or "falling in love", is true love; for it is only when couples fall out of love that the real work of sacrificial love can begin.

Of course, the great Doctors of the Church have known and taught this for centuries. Life is not about perpetual exhilaration, and love is not about feeling good. Life is about God, and love is about sacrifice. It is about loving the other not for what he or she does for me, but for the others' own sake. Love involves an exit of self, a loss of self, a forgetting of self.

But all this has to be taught, and it has to be practiced so as to become a habit. It has to be taught in the family; for it is not being taught on a cultural level.

One cannot love one's neighbor (including one's spouse) without first loving God above all things. The most important prayer in Israel was The Shema: "Hear, O Israel! The Lord is our God, the Lord alone! Therefore, you shall love the Lord, your God, with all your heart, and with all your soul, and with all your strength" (Dt 6, 4-5).

Clearly, we live in the midst of a wounded culture, one that has lost a sense of history, not to mention a religious sense. It will take years, decades, possibly centuries to heal such a culture, but the way to do it is through the family. This is what Israel has taught all other nations, like a firstborn son teaches his younger siblings. This gospel is an illustration of just what happens when a mother and a father fulfill what is their primary duty.

Christianity arose out of Judaism. Like Judaism, Christianity is a historical religion. It is about a covenant, a new covenant, sealed in Christ's blood, and Christ commanded us to eat his body and drink his blood in remembrance of him. It is about a Person, a divine Person, who actually entered into history, to reveal the face of God the Father and to reconcile man to God by the shedding of his blood. He came to cancel the debt of sin and to rise from the dead so that we might have eternal life.

The cultural heritage of the Church is as rich as Judaism; we too have a liturgical year that is all about keeping memories alive, the memory of Christ's birth, the Epiphany, his entry into Jerusalem, his passion, death, and resurrection, and the descent of the Holy Spirit upon the Church. Our feast days that celebrate specific saints are about knowing them, remembering them, taking what they gave us and bringing it into our own household. And the primary duty of a father of a Catholic household is to pass down this rich Catholic heritage to his children. That comes before everything. And the primary duty of a Catholic mother is to teach her children the faith. But we cannot give what we do not have, and so we have to come to know our faith, to know that heritage, in order to pass it on. If we don't, our children are going to be molded by an irreligious culture that puts the worship of the self at the center, not the worship of God, which is why we see so many young men calling it quits, getting up and packing their bags, leaving their wives to take care of the children all by themselves, because they don't feel fulfilled or didn't think that marriage was going to be so difficult and demanding.

We can do so much good for future generations if we begin now. Just as the Jews have visible and tangible signs, i.e., tefillin, pushke, siddur and machzor, prayer shawls, kosher dishes, kosher foods, a structured prayer life, so too do Catholics. Our roots are there, in Israel. We have sacraments and sacramentals, visible devotions, like the Rosary, the Chaplet of the Divine Mercy, both with a history behind them, other prayer chaplets, scapulars, holy medals of saints, traditional prayers, litanies, different spiritualities from saints of entirely different personalities, the writings of the great saints, classic biographies of saints, etc.

The best thing we can do to heal this culture is to learn the Catholic faith, immerse ourselves into this cultural heritage, create a profoundly religious atmosphere in our home. Make sure you have a crucifix in every room, a real crucifix with a corpus, have statues of saints in the home, your favorite saints, the ones you identify with. And of course we have to study the lives of the saints. Parents have to learn the teachings of the Church, especially in key areas such as the moral teachings of the Church, particularly in the area of marriage and sexuality, since that is virtually non-existent in this culture, which is one reason why there is so much marriage break up. And they have to teach their children to sacrifice, teach them what love is and how to love, to think of the poor before themselves, teach them the corporal and spiritual works of mercy, etc.

If we create such a culture in the home for our children, we may not live to see the results, but the Lord will certainly make known to us the incalculable good that our parenting has done for civilization, and He will thank us for our service, and it will be an eternal thanks which all the saints will behold, because God is eternal and all will be revealed in heaven.

11. Creating Domestic Anchors

One of the great achievements of modern psychology is a more precise understanding of the unconscious mind and the many ways that our judgments and decisions are unconsciously influenced by outside factors. Anchoring is a cognitive bias that, for the most part, we are unaware of. The bias is that we have a tendency to rely too heavily on the first piece of information we are given when making decisions or judgments. To demonstrate this to students, I will show them a picture of a stack of old and rare books and all they have to do is circle whether or not they believe the books are worth more than $100 or less than $100. They will circle what they think, and then they are asked to estimate the total worth of the books. We then add up the total numbers and divide by 30 students (or by however many students there are) to get the average. We then show them how much their average differed from another class that was given the same picture, only they were asked whether they believed the total cost was more than $800 or less than $800. The students of that class were also asked to circle what they believed and to estimate the total cost of the books. The class average of the latter was always significantly higher, because they were unconsciously influenced by the mention of $800, while the other was unconsciously influenced by the mere mention of $100.

Salesmen are aware of this and use it to their advantage. I traded in my car one year, and the dealer offered to give me $4000 for it. I thought that was a bit low, so he asked me what I thought was reasonable. I did not do my homework beforehand, so on the spot I thought perhaps $6000 was reasonable. He left for 15 minutes, came back and said it was a battle, but his boss finally agreed: $6000 it is. When I told a friend of mine this, he looked up the value of the make, model and year and said I should have received $10,000 for it, and they would have sold it for

$13,000. He anchored me low; I was influenced by the $4000 and did not want to stray too far from that number, just as the students were unconsciously influenced by the request to decide whether the books were over 100 or under 100. If they thought they were worth more, they were unwilling to estimate much more than that.

Why do I bring this up? Because there are all sorts of anchors that influence us in ways we are not explicitly aware of. There are cultural anchors, and many of them are moral anchors, which are culturally accepted standards, and today the moral anchors of contemporary popular culture are very low, but so few of us are aware of it. What we are aware of, however, are the cultural anchors of a past era. We look back to centuries of slavery in Christian Europe and are astounded that people (including the hierarchy) could have tolerated slavery for so long. However, people were just as subject to cultural moral anchors (and other cognitive constraints) then as we are today, it's just that when we are outside the influence of the anchor, our vision is much clearer (hindsight is 20/20). So in a few hundred years from now, a generation will be looking back at us today, shaking their heads at what we are currently tolerating and failing to do; it's hard to say exactly what this will and will not include.

But how do we go about changing this cultural depravity and moving society along towards a more civilized and humane world? I ask this because when we begin to feel how little we are in this vast world, we begin to despair that we can do much to influence things for the better. The temptation is to capitulate. But there is a way, and it is a small way, but it is the only way forward. I'm referring to the creation of domestic anchors—the moral anchors that are established in the context of the family.

The reason I find teaching to be such a delight at this time is that my students come from very solid immigrant families. Their parents, for the most part, have not allowed themselves to be too influenced by contemporary culture. They discipline their kids, they eat with their kids, they teach their kids, they leisure with them, love them, and so those kids have not been emotionally neglected. Hence, our students are generally happy and can concentrate on school. A good number of these parents exhibit a genuine moral integrity, and so there is a very high moral anchor in the home. As a result, the students are not terribly influenced by the low moral anchor of the culture outside the home. But if a family crumbles, or should the parents fail in their duty to be inspiring models for their children, the only anchor left for children is the very permissive and low moral anchor of the culture—and picking out who those kids are is often an easy thing to do.

The latest in neurology corroborates this point on the importance of parenthood. The proper development of a child's brain depends significantly on the mother and how she relates to her child. A psychologically healthy mother will intuitively know not to overstimulate her child, nor will she under-stimulate the child through emotional neglect. There are mirror neurons in the brain that line up with the neural circuitry of the mother, permitting the baby to feel what the mother feels. The human emotions are contagious precisely because of these mirror neurons. We are very influenced by the emotions of others, and this is especially true of the child and his or her mother. When parenting fails, the repercussions, beginning with the neurological effects on the child, are far reaching; but when couples parent well, they influence their child's entire neurological development in ways they are probably not aware of.

The nobility of the institution of the family cannot be acknowledged any more emphatically by the Church than Her decision to situate the feast of the Holy Family right after Christmas day. This is a season of hope and light, and the family is the hope of civilization. Parenting is the most important work, and that's how civilization is moved forward. We don't hear that anymore, but there is no vocation that has greater importance; everything is at the service of the family (the Church is at the service of family, so too the economy as well as education, etc.). The task of parents is to do the little that has been entrusted to them, to focus on their spouses and children and to become persons of the highest possible moral and psychological integrity for the sake of their children. What happens after that is in God's hands, not ours. There is no doubt that children might very well turn away and allow themselves to be influenced by the low cultural anchors out there, but like any anchor, they tend not to veer too far from the domestic anchor that was theirs growing up. So that's our task, and it is a profoundly important one.

12. Disordered Passion and Obedience

*Where do the wars and where do the conflicts among you
come from? Is it not from your passions that make war within
your members?* (Jm 4,1)

What is interesting about the quote above from the
Letter of James is that it locates the source of social
disorder not in the structure of government or in political
mechanisms, but in the disordered passions of individual
persons. Today, the tendency is to believe that the source
of our social problems is in systems of government, and
not the disordered appetites and deficient character of
individual persons. What is also interesting to consider is
that the founding fathers of the United States always
maintained that virtuous persons alone make good
government possible, and that without virtuous citizens,
good government, whose end is social order, is impossible.

One of the effects of Original Sin is the disorder or
rebellion of the passions. There are eleven basic passions of
the sensitive appetites. Specifically, the passions are
appetitive reactions that follow upon knowledge. The
passions of the pleasure appetite are love, desire,
satisfaction, hate, aversion and sorrow; the passions of the
aggressive appetite are hope, despair, fear, daring, and
anger. Animals are governed by their passions, but human
beings are to be governed by a higher faculty, namely
reason and will power. The passions become fully human
when they are given proper order by a will that is subject to
reason, that is, when they are disposed to obey the demands
of reason. The emotions have an innate need to be guided
by reason, and without being so guided, emotional health is
not possible, much less a healthy and well-ordered civil
community.

But disposing the emotions to obey reason is a very
difficult thing to accomplish because of the wound of

Original Sin, and it takes years of hard work and suffering to bring to the passions that kind of order. But that's what the virtues are: they are habits that dispose the passions to obey reason.

The interesting thing about the passions is that they affect the way we see the world, and so if our passions are disordered, the way we see the world will be distorted as well. As a person grows in virtue, he begins to see through the clear lenses of a well ordered character; but if he refuses to grow in virtue, he remains emotionally immature, and the result is a skewed and distorted mind.

So why is it that so many people refuse to cultivate the virtues? Why is bringing the emotions of the pleasure appetite under the governance of reason so unpopular? Why is it that so many people today don't know what the word "temperance" means—which Aristotle defines as the virtue that moderates the pleasures of touch? Why is chastity so unpopular, on a cultural level at least? Why are so many people today impulsive? The reason is that cultivating virtue is hard work. It involves personal sacrifice, and it is more important for people today to "feel" a certain way than to "be a certain kind of person" (a person of good moral character). Emotions are about "feeling", but character is about "being"—good character is about being a certain kind of person", one with a morally beautiful identity. But to be a person of moral nobility requires a willingness to make sacrifices, to do without, to control oneself, to obey a higher law, for the sake of the common good, which includes my own good, but is larger than it.

Frankly, this culture places the emphasis on feeling, not character. And so an increasing number of people today choose for the sake of their own pleasure, rather than out of a love for the common good and obedience to the moral order. And so petty theft is more common today, as is lying, perjury, insurance fraud, cheating, and indulgence of all kinds.

The problem is that disordered passion blinds the intellect, which in turn leads to imprudent decisions, very often unjust decisions, and these in turn have very costly social repercussions. One morning I was driving to work, trying to think of examples for my students that illustrate how disordered passion blinds the mind. I was stopped at an intersection with a red light; I was about to turn right, but the oncoming cars had an advanced green, and one is not permitted by law to turn right on a red light with an advanced green. As I am waiting for the light to turn green, and a young man in an SUV behind me begins to lean on his horn. I simply point to the oncoming cars and shrug my shoulders. But he continues to press on the horn. I ignore it. When the light turns green, he steps on the pedal, speeds past me, cuts me off and slams on his breaks, almost causing a collision, he then waves his fist. I'm somewhat in shock at this point. He drives off, but at the next red light, I take down his license number and later file a Road Watch report. I'm not sure if it accomplished anything, but what I found interesting is that this man had no idea who I was. I could have been a sociopath, a person with a long criminal record. I could have been a complete "nutcase" with a gun looking for an excuse to make someone's life miserable— and there are plenty of those kinds of people around today. He wasn't able to consider this. Vehement passion blinded his mind. Lucky for him it was a Deacon who was a religion teacher trying to think of a way to explain how disordered passion blinds the mind. I had my illustration for the students that day.

Only one week later, the same thing happened on a major intersection in my home town. It was early in the morning, just before leaving for school, I had just finished telling my wife: "If someone is driving like a crazy nut, don't honk the horn. There are a lot of adults out there who are not all there mentally and emotionally." I should have taken my own advice; not ten minutes later a lady was on my bumper, so when the street became two lanes, I moved to the right lane immediately, but the woman speeds past me, only an inch from the side of my car. I made the decision to give the horn a little toot. That was a mistake! She pulled in front of me, slammed on her brakes, and stuck her arm out the window with one of her fingers pointing to the sky. This time I didn't bother with Road Watch—I thought the police would begin to question whether or not there is something wrong with me. But once again this is a good illustration of how disordered passion blinds the intellect. I could have been some narcissist who despises women; I could have followed her to work, followed her home, or waited till she got to a red light, etc. She had given a stranger the excuse he might have been looking for to rise up out of his boredom and wreak havoc upon her life, under the guise of justice. She didn't think; she just reacted impulsively.

I was even sitting in a Mr. Greek Express one evening waiting for my order to take out and there was a family sitting down having supper. The father called the waitress over and very aggressively demanded to see the manager. She approached. Holding his knife in his hand, waving it about, he spoke to her as if she had just committed the most heinous crime. It was really quite frightening to watch, my heart rate rapidly increased just witnessing this. The injustice was that his wife's order got mixed up: she'd ordered chicken, not pork, or something to that effect.

There is another example of how the disordered love of food—and a corresponding inability to tolerate any kind of sorrow brought on by delay—affects the mind. In other words, what is not an injustice at all is judged to be a serious violation of justice, which in turn gives rise to vehement anger. Compare that reaction to the person with an ordered appetite for food who simply calls the waitress over and politely points out the mistake and waits. Nobody's day is ruined.

What disordered passion also does is that it blinds us to the limits of our own perspective. We are not aware of just how limited our point of view is—we tend to think our purview is much larger and more comprehensive than it actually is; we "feel" right, and so we fail to listen to others, we dismiss them or demonize them (we see this in politics all the time). But as we get older, we should begin to see that reality is much more complex than we once thought, and we are not so "passionate" (self-righteous) anymore. At least that's what should happen. Very often it does not, because of pride, which is the disordered emotion of love bearing on one's own excellence. One cannot tolerate the feeling of being wrong—it conflicts with one's rather inflated image of oneself. And so if one insists on enjoying the feeling of being one up on others, then one is unwilling to listen and have one's viewpoint enlarged. The unfortunate result is that one does not get to experience the real joy of a richer possession of reality; instead, one settles for a feeling that is based on an illusion.

In the gospel, the Apostles, the very foundation stones of the Church, are arguing amongst themselves, discussing who among them is the greatest. Hence, the disordered emotion of self-esteem. What is strange, however, is that Jesus calls over a child. I say it is strange because children are governed by their passions, and the problem with the Apostles is that they were behaving like emotionally immature children.

Of course, that's not the aspect that Jesus is calling attention to in the child. One of the most wonderful characteristics of the child is "openness": a child is open to learning. It is only later on, in adulthood, that some people will make the decision to close themselves, because they have decided that feeling emotionally complacent is more important than the continual improvement of one's character.

Every ten years or so there usually appears on the best seller list a New Age book of some kind. In the 70s it was *The Power of Positive Thinking*, later on it was *The Celestine Prophecy*, then came Deepak Chopra, then *The Secret*, etc., and what all these New Age books have in common is they promise that if we think a certain way, the forces of the universe will somehow converge upon us in a positive way and we will prosper. What's interesting, however, is that there does not seem to be any call to personal reform, no need to obey commandments, etc. Salvation without moral reform, without the need to cultivate virtue or make painful sacrifices; rather, we can live on our own terms.

I believe that the most fundamental virtue is obedience: obedience to the natural moral law, obedience to the divine law, obedience to the Law of Christ, and that's the one thing that people find the most difficult, and so they very often convince themselves that they can have a close relationship with God on their terms, without reforming themselves morally.

We are called to be perpetually open to truth, in particular moral truth, to the demands of the natural moral law. We are called to be continually open to the never ending improvement of our character, which means we have to have the willingness and fortitude to behold our own moral deficiencies, to discover them, moral deficiencies that often others see but we do not. If we live in a childlike spirit of openness and obedience, with a willingness to be measured by a reality larger than ourselves, regardless of how it might make us feel at first, we will grow in a genuine spirit of happiness, a happiness that is much deeper and richer than the fleeting pleasures that so many people settle for.

13. Euthanasia and the Sanctity of Life Ethic

Over the past 40 years, there have been subtle changes in the way we as a culture regard human life. There seems to be one of two possible postures one can take that bear upon the value of individual human life. The first is the Sanctity of Life Mentality, which at one time dominated the medical profession, and the other is the Quality of Life Mentality, which seems to be more widespread today.

The Sanctity of Life Mentality regards individual human life as holy (created by God), sacred (set apart), of immeasurable value (not infinite value), regardless of the physical and/or mental quality of the person. You can place a price on things, but not on human persons who are created by God and who are called by God, each one individually, to union with Him in the unimaginable joy of eternal life.

The Quality of Life Mentality does not see individual human life as holy, sacred, of immeasurable value, but actually places a value on individual human life on the basis of its physical and/or mental quality, as we would price a product. We value computers and automobiles on the basis of their quality, whether they function well, are useful, efficient, etc. The Quality of Life Mentality places a higher value on a human life that is of higher physical and mental quality, and a lesser value on individual human life that is of lesser physical and mental quality. And so a handicapped child would be of less value than a healthy child.

In this framework, human persons are valued for their productivity or ability to be of some use to society. They are not valued (loved) for their own sake, but for the sake of what they can do for society as a whole.

The Christian world has always rejected this. Every individual person has been created by God, and God created each one of us for Himself, not for our parents, and not for the State, but for eternal union with Himself, because He loves us individually, and He loves us as if there is only one of us. He entrusts human beings (children) to parents, but they belong to God first and foremost. Of course God calls us all to serve others, but each person here has been given life for his/her own sake. And Christ is mysteriously united to every individual person here, because we have been created by God and that same God joined a human nature, like ours, and with that nature redeemed us. Christ sacrifices himself so that we might have life; but those who belong to the culture of death have the reverse attitude: in principle they believe one may sacrifice individual human life in order to make their own temporary lives here more convenient (i.e., abortion).

This attitude of the culture of death spread rapidly after the legalization of abortion, and many social critics predicted that infanticide would soon follow, which is the deliberate starvation and neglect of handicapped children whose lives are deemed not worth living, and of course we saw this come to pass in the famous Baby Doe case back in April of 1982 in Bloomington, Indiana. Infanticide has been happening ever since, here as well as in the Netherlands.

Critics also pointed out that the next target, after infants, will be the terminally ill and the elderly. To help this along, we have seen a gradual redefining of terms, in particular murder. The western world has always understood murder to be the intentional killing of another human being; that the murdered victim wanted to die was and is entirely irrelevant. If I shoot someone who asked to be shot, that he willed it does not change the fact that I carried out an act with the will (intent) to bring an end to his life, which is fundamentally good. That is murderous.

What is happening today is that murder is being defined as killing another against his/her will. We of course do not accept this. My will does not alter the value of my life. Human life itself is intrinsically good whether the person is sick, or terminally ill and dying, whether he wants to live or not, whether he is mentally ill, depressed, or mentally handicapped, or quadriplegic, etc.

There are two types of euthanasia: active and passive. Active euthanasia is death by commission. The person is given a lethal injection, for example, or the doctor mixes up a cocktail that the patient drinks, which of course will kill him. Passive euthanasia is death by omission. A person dies because a certain medical treatment is omitted or withdrawn. Active euthanasia is never justified, because it always amounts to murder; for it is the intentional destruction of human life, which as was said is intrinsically good and of immeasurable value, regardless of the condition of the patient. Passive euthanasia, however, can at times be justified, depending on the circumstances. Here is where we have to be very careful. At this point we need to distinguish between two types of treatment, namely, extraordinary treatment and ordinary treatment. Extraordinary treatment is any medical treatment that is a serious burden on the patient, physically, psychologically, emotionally, or even financially. Ordinary treatment is any medical treatment that is not a serious burden on the patient, physically, or psychologically, or emotionally, or financially.

Traditional medical ethics and Catholic teaching have always taught that one is obligated to use ordinary treatment to preserve human life, but one is not obligated to use extraordinary treatment to preserve human life. Some examples at this point might help. If a treatment is a serious burden on the patient in one of the aforementioned ways and he refuses it because it is seriously burdensome, he is not necessarily willing (intending) his own death; rather, he might only be accepting (permitting) his death as a side effect of refusing a seriously burdensome treatment. Suppose a doctor were to tell you that you have six months to live, but that with a treatment which carries painful side effects, or psychologically repugnant ones that are serious, you can extend your life for an extra two years or so. A person does not necessarily have an obligation to consent to it. If the treatment is a serious financial burden on a person, for example, he or she does not necessarily have a duty to consent to the treatment.

Again, what the person wills in refusing treatment is not necessarily the destruction of his own life, but the ending or impeding of a medical treatment that is seriously burdensome in some way. Death is a side effect of removing a burdensome treatment, and death is accepted, not intended.

But some people omit ordinary treatment so that the patient will die. We saw this in Missouri with the Nancy Cruzan case. The parents pushed to have the feeding tube removed, not because it was burdensome, but because they couldn't stand to see their daughter in that condition— understandably so. The tube was removed so that she would die. Her death was willed as a means to an end. This is murderous, however polite and well meaning.

We need to be careful of what some call extraordinary treatment. High tech medical equipment is not necessarily extraordinary treatment. The definition of extraordinary is such that what is ordinary here in Canada might very well be extraordinary in the United States. As circumstances change, so too might the status of a medical treatment. What is ordinary treatment for a young 40 year old, such as a relatively mild form of chemo therapy, might constitute extraordinary treatment for a 77 year old man whose body may not be able to recover as well as the younger man. Performing CPR on a young teenager whose heart has stopped is usually ordinary treatment—a young man can recover from the injuries to his rib cage resulting from CPR, but an 86 year old grandmother who has already been resuscitated once before might find the physical side effects of CPR far too burdensome. Her decision in favour of a

DNR order is not necessarily suicidal; rather she might very well be accepting her death, not necessarily willing it; rather, she wills or intends to be delivered from a treatment that she finds seriously burdensome physically. So, she says: "if I am having a heart attack, it's my time to go, so let me go." That's very different from removing all treatment because one does not wish to live with a disease or does not want a child who is disabled.

Those who promote euthanasia will often use the expression "serious burden" within the context of their discussion. If we look closely at what exactly is the serious burden, however, we often see that it is not the medical treatment that is burdensome, but the condition of the patient. It is never justified to intentionally destroy human life in order to relieve one of a burdensome existence; that is to do evil to achieve good.

Our obligation is to love our patients, not for our sake, but for theirs, to care for them even when they cannot thank us or when they are not apparently aware of us. Our duty is to make them as comfortable as possible. We may use pain management that may, as an undesirable side effect, shorten a person's life. In this case, we accept that side effect. But we must not eliminate the pain by intentionally eliminating the patient.

14. Exercising One's Priesthood in Dying

I didn't think it would take as long as it did for the Supreme Court of Canada to arrive at the decision to permit "doctor assisted suicide". When a principle is laid down, it is only a matter of time before the logical implications of that principle are unravelled, and the principle was laid down much earlier when abortion was made legal in this country. Many predicted this would lead to infanticide, and this is just what happened in the early 80s in the United States, and that too has come to Canada.

The ethics of "doctor assisted suicide" is not that complex, and the letter from the Canadian Conference of Catholic Bishops gets to the heart of the matter: "[A]n act or omission which, of itself or by intention, causes death in order to eliminate suffering constitutes a murder gravely contrary to the dignity of the human person and to the respect due to the living God, our Creator."

The Supreme Court decision, however, is frightening from a theological point of view. A chaplain once said to me that death bed conversions are rare; people generally die as they live. If they lived without God, typically they die without God. But, if they lived a life of prayer, if they have the habit of prayer, if they know the Lord and have made Him the center of their lives, He becomes the center of their death as well. Psalm 116 says "Precious in the eyes of the Lord is the death of his servant". Death is our final act; it becomes a holy act, a final and definitive prayer in fact, when we join our suffering and our death to the suffering and death of Christ. Our death becomes an offering. We were anointed priest, prophet, and king at baptism, and at death, we get to exercise our office of priesthood in the act of dying, by offering ourselves and our entire life to God. The legalization of doctor assisted suicide will now allow others, who might not be as strong in their faith, to turn their final act, their act of dying, into an act of murder; a final act of rebellion.

If this life is all there is, if the purpose of our life is simply to enjoy it, to experience the pleasures and the goods of this world, then doctor assisted suicide makes perfect sense. We take our pets to the vet to get them euthanized; we don't have funerals for them, nor do we have Masses said for them. The life of a brute animal is all about the pleasures of eating, sleeping, and mating.

But this life is not all there is, and the purpose of this life is not pleasure. This life is a preparation for eternal life; this life is about learning how to love God. The Second Person of the Trinity joined a human nature in order to show us what it means to be man, and the purpose of our life is to make of it an offering to God. This life is a way of the cross. He said: "Anyone who wishes to be a follower of mine, let him take up his cross and follow me". Follow him where? To Calvary. Our life and our final act, our death, must become an offering to God. In death, we do not die alone; rather, we die in the Person of Christ. We discover him in this life to the degree that we die to ourselves, and we find him completely by turning our final act into an act of prayer.

It's very hard to convince people without faith that euthanasia is wrong. If they lack faith in the Person of Christ, they see no meaning in suffering. All we are left with now are abstract philosophical arguments against it, and that does not compel those who are suffering. But just as Christ's suffering and death brought salvation to the world and allowed divine grace to flow once again through the veins of humanity, so to speak, so too the death of a person who has joined his life and death to Christ merits graces for others in ways that we simply cannot conceive of at this point. Part of their joy in heaven will be the discovery of just how much their sufferings have brought grace and blessing to others. Christ redeems us by suffering and dying, and if we want to be a part of his victory, if we want to have a share in his work of salvation, there is only one way, and it is to follow him to Calvary. Those without faith can't make sense out of that; all this, in fact, sounds like gibberish. But to those of us with faith, we understand it. We know it. We live it.

In this gospel that we heard today (Mt 8, 2), the leper shows tremendous faith when he says to Jesus: "If you choose, you can make me clean". Jesus is moved by such faith and responds: "'Of course I choose. Be made clean'. Then Jesus stretched out his hand and touched him".

It is the touch of Christ that heals. It is the touch of Christ that forgives sin and that strengthens us now and especially in our dying. In other words, it is the Eucharist that is our strength now and at the moment of our death. If you've made the Eucharist the center of your life, you are going to die well, because we die as we live. There is nothing to fear in death when you are dying in union with Christ. His strength will be your strength.

My good friend, a priest of a nearby diocese, anoints a lot of people during the year, and it has been his experience that when he gives the Eucharist to a dying patient who has loved the Eucharist all his life, the patient will often say something like "Don't let me hold you up, Father, you have all sorts of things to do". At those moments, my friend is keenly aware that he is not needed anymore. He's a well beloved priest, but they don't want him around, because they have all they need; they have who they need. There is nothing more for him to do but leave. Although it is the priest (or deacon) who dismisses the faithful at the end of Mass, now it is the one dying who dismisses the priest who brought him Christ in the Eucharist. Christ alone comforts them in their final moments of dying, so much so that any added efforts on the part of the priest or deacon to bring comfort to the dying is very often more of a nuisance than a source of comfort.

The moment of death comes for us all, and that is the most important moment of our lives. Let us not be afraid of it, for although it will involve suffering, in the midst of that suffering we will find what all the martyrs found, which is the joy and presence of Christ in the deepest region of our spirit, where no pain and suffering can touch us.

15. Some Thoughts on Homosexuality, Happiness, and Character

It is important to point out that the homosexual orientation is not a matter of character or personality any more than heterosexuality is. Personality describes a particular combination of emotional, attitudinal, and behavioral response patterns in a person. As such, one's personality is the result of environmental as well as genetic factors. Two people of entirely opposite sexual orientations can have very similar personalities, i.e., outgoing, extroverted, or highly introverted, prone to anxiety, etc.

Character, on the other hand, is one's moral identity; it is our deepest identity that we have shaped for ourselves as a result of the moral choices we've made. Whatever is not a matter of choice has no part in the determination of our character. Thus, the homosexual orientation is not a matter of character, for one does not choose to have a homosexual orientation any more than one chooses to have a heterosexual orientation. And so, three different people, each one possessing a homosexual orientation, can have three entirely different characters; one might be a saint, the other a narcissist, and the other a morally upright citizen, etc.

The homosexual orientation, like the heterosexual orientation, is neither a personality trait nor a character trait; it is, rather, an inclination, a propensity, that is, an appetite. Happiness is not a matter of appetite, not for anyone, whether heterosexual or homosexual. Rather, happiness is a matter of character. Happiness is the result of the kind of character that one has established by virtue of the moral choices one has made, and so a person with a homosexual orientation has just as much opportunity for a genuinely happy life as a person with a heterosexual orientation.

But just as a heterosexual who simply pursues the satisfaction of his appetites in life inevitably finds himself frustrated in his pursuit of happiness, so too the person with a homosexual orientation will be frustrated in his or her pursuit of happiness as long as he or she confuses happiness with the satisfaction of the appetites.

The fact of the matter is that every one of us has inordinate appetites to contend with. Some of us have to battle against inordinate self-esteem (pride), or inordinate love of our own good to the exclusion of others (envy); some of us struggle with an inordinate love of possessing (avarice), while some of us battle inordinate anger. Some have to battle an inordinate love of rest and an aversion to exertion (sloth), others an inordinate love of food and drink, while others have to battle inordinate sexual desire. Our salvation is not found in the satisfaction of those inordinate appetites, but rather in the successful victory over ourselves and our own inordinate propensities. And sometimes it takes a lifetime of experience for people to learn that lesson; others, for some reason, figure it out early in life.

The reason that happiness is found in a victory over the self is that happiness is a matter of character—"being" a certain kind of person, as opposed to "having" certain kinds of experiences. It is not the world, or this person or that person, who is my own worst enemy; rather, I am my own worst enemy—my own disordered propensities are my own worst enemy. The most fundamental need of the human person is the need to love and be loved. This is another way of saying that the most fundamental need of the human person is to be important. Each human person has a fundamental importance, and most of us, if not all of us, have no idea just how important we really are. And the reason for this is that we have not been loved enough in life—most people in our lives, whose responsibility it was to love us, confuse passion for love and have thus loved themselves too much, and us too little; and we seem to continue the cycle.

But love is not a passion; love is an act of the will. The need to be important is really a need "exist for", because to be important is to be important "for" someone or others. And so the need to love and be loved translates into 1) the need to "exist for" (which means the need to love) and 2) the need to know I "exist for" (which means I know that I am important for someone or others and thus loved). Thus, only knowing creatures (persons) can be happy, for if I "exist for", but am not aware that I "exist for" because I lack intellectual self-consciousness, then I cannot be happy (a building is not happy or unhappy).

As was said, love is not a passion, but an act of the will. Now all love involves a kind of self-expansion. For example, to love and consume food brings about physical growth, sexual desire usually results in reproductive expansion (pregnancy), etc. But love as an act of the will is the only love that is specifically human, for the human person is a moral agent, for he alone has a will (a rational appetite). To love another human being "humanly" is to will the good of that person as another self. In other words, just as I naturally will the best for myself, I can also freely choose to will the best for that person for his sake, not for my sake. The passion of love is not capable of that level of self-transcendence, for the passions are sensitive appetitive reactions and they terminate in the self. For example, to have a passion for chocolate is to love chocolate not for the sake of the chocolate, but for my sake; I love it for what it does for me (it brings me pleasure).

Happiness is not a matter of pleasure, as human beings have known for centuries; consider ancient Hinduism's four stages of happiness; pleasure is the first and lowest stage. We find the same insight in Buddhism, Taoism, Socrates, Plato and Aristotle, etc. The only happiness of which brute animals are capable is the happiness of pleasure. But man is more than a brute animal, which is why a life of sensual satisfaction is insufficient for the human person. People always eventually seek more than that. Human happiness is a matter of the self-expansion that results from the specifically human kind of love, which is agape. If I love this other as another self (for his sake), then I am no longer one, but two. And if I love a third person as another self (for his or her sake), then I am no longer two, but three, etc. The more people I love as another self, for their sake and not my own, the larger I become (we are not talking about physical size), and the larger I become, the happier I will be. The reason is that happiness is a matter of goodness, and "good" is a property of being. The larger I am, the better I am. God, who is Goodness Itself, is Happiness Itself (Joy Itself). The larger a person is, the more like God he or she is and thus the happier he or she is.

And so, can those persons with a homosexual orientation ever be happy? Of course they can, just as much as those with a heterosexual orientation. But not everyone with a heterosexual orientation is happy, and the reason has nothing to do with their sexual orientation; it has everything to do with their moral identity (character), that is, the kind of persons they have made themselves to be by the choices that they are making. Not every heterosexual is committed to virtue; many in fact live for the satisfaction of their passions. As well, there are many who have a homosexual orientation and are very happy, because they have freely chosen to orientate their lives towards their true and eternal end, which is union with God in the Beatific Vision, God who is Goodness Itself, Truth Itself, and Beauty Itself. The very fact that they have chosen to forgo the satisfaction of their sexual orientation for the sake of the virtue of chastity is not a hindrance to their well-being and happiness any more than celibacy and chastity is a hindrance to the happiness of a Mother Theresa or a St. Francis of Assisi.

The notion that happiness is about the fulfillment of one's desire for a sexually intimate relationship with another is a confusion that has its source not in the homosexual community as such, but in the culture at large, and so this discourse on happiness is not primarily for those with a homosexual orientation, but any and all human persons of whatever orientation they may be required to do battle with. But the first thing we need to see is that there is a battle to be fought; each one of us is called to bring about order within the self (to cultivate the virtues) for the sake of something larger, and doing so takes a very long time and involves personal sacrifice. But the purpose of bringing order to the passions is that we may direct our lives towards the common good of the social whole and most importantly our ultimate end, which is eternal union with God. But disorder in the passions renders those ends very difficult if not impossible to achieve; for there is no just social order (justice) without virtuous persons. A person of virtue has chosen to love the common good more than his private good, and happiness is to be found only in persons of such character, and character has to do not so much with our own particular battle ground as it does with how we choose to relate to it. Most people, regardless of sexual orientation, will choose to go only so far in that battle and will often reserve some small area of disordered delight for themselves, whether that involves a degree of pride, unforgiveness, love of possessing, sloth, gluttony or lust. My role is not to appease such people, but to challenge them to something higher, a brighter, loftier, and more joyful existence that can only be known from within by being freely chosen and lived.

16. Humility

I recall driving through the mountains of upstate New York with a friend of mine who teaches chemistry. It was during the March Break, and so there was a great deal of snow still on the mountains. As he was looking out at the snow, he remarked: "The most powerful force in nature". I asked him: "What is the most powerful force in nature?" He said: "Water". He continued: "When the weather gets warm, all that snow will turn into water and it is all going downhill".

And it is true; water is the most powerful force in nature, more powerful than fire, and more powerful than wind. Water can take a huge bulldozer or an 18 wheeler and toss it along as if it were a twig. But water always seeks the lowest place. If there is a leak in the roof, the water slowly makes its way to the lowest place, the basement, and soon the basement is flooded.

Water is a perfect symbol of God, for God is the most powerful; there is no limit to His power. There is nothing God cannot do. And yet He became flesh and dwelt among us. And He, like water, sought the lowest place. He was born in a stable among smelly brute animals and excluded from the comforts of an Inn. He was born into a poor family: Joseph offered turtledoves in place of a lamb, at the Presentation, because that was the offering of a poor man. Christ said: "Foxes have holes, birds have nests, but the Son of Man has nowhere to lay his head". And he died on a cross, totally humiliated and rejected.

God is like water, He seeks the lowest place. And God continues to seek the lowest place; He dwells in humble souls; He chooses to make His home in the souls of those who feel worthless, who feel they are nothing, who are neglected, who feel unimportant, souls to whom no one pays any attention. That is where God is comfortable, so to speak, in the souls of the humble.

So when you feel unimportant, when you feel forgotten, when you feel that you are nothing, that you are worthless, when you feel terribly sick and in darkness, rejoice in the depths of your soul because you have become the dwelling place of the Most High God. Delight in the fact that you have the honor of housing the Almighty in the hiddenness of your soul. And if you are a nurse, keep in mind that the patients that you serve have the honor of housing the Almighty, and however you choose to treat them, that is the measure of your love of God—or your lack of love, depending on how much patience, care, and reverence you show them.

17. Looking at Us Through Rose Colored Glasses

It is always interesting to consider just how much the emotions affect our judgment. They can distort judgment, and they can also sharpen our judgment, i.e., in emergency situations. Think about someone who has fallen in love; she sees the beloved everywhere; everything reminds her of the person she has fallen in love with. You could say that falling in love brings about a kind of "psychosis": the person is no longer completely in touch with reality. The expressions we use to describe someone who is in love testify to this: "She's on cloud nine", which might imply she's no longer aware of her surroundings; or, "She sees him through rose colored glasses".

There's something to this experience, however. I believe it has a theological meaning, minus all the imperfections associated with it. Allow me to explain. God the Son joined a human nature; he is like us in all things but sin; he came to establish his kingdom, and he did so by dying; his death is the perfect offering of Himself to the Father, on our behalf. The shedding of his blood is a ransom, a payoff, as it were; he offers his life to pay a debt that is too great for us to pay—this is one very limited way of looking at it. He is God, and so what he offers is perfect and of infinite value; and he is man. As man, he can act on our behalf. The Father sees him, so to speak, sees his offering, and is pleased with his offering because behind it is a perfect love, the love of God the Son. The resurrection is the acceptance of that offering, the final proof that the debt of sin has been paid for.

We are now in God's favor, precisely because of that perfect sacrificial offering. When God the Father sees you and me, He sees His Son, because He loves His Son; there is nothing the Father loves more than His Son, and when

His Son became flesh, He did not cease to be God the Son. He is God the Son in the flesh. He is one of us, our brother, a son of man, and because of that, the Father now sees His Son when he sees us. There's a sense in which God the Father looks at us through rose colored glasses.

We are now in His favor, and to be in a state of grace is to be in God's favor. We don't have to remain in His favor, we can choose to walk out of that favor; but the point is, when God sees us, He sees a likeness of His Son, and he delights in us as a result of that. It's like you loving your grandchildren, because you see your own son in the faces of your grandchildren.

More to the point, however, when God the Father sees us suffer, He sees his Son in the depths of our suffering. When we experience our radical frailty, our limitations, when the world feels too overwhelming and we taste our helplessness, He sees His Son in us because it was through that kind of an experience that the Son saved us, redeemed us, made up for our lovelessness through a perfect act of divine and human love. In fact, anyone who experiences the alienation and emptiness that results from choosing sin, that's when the Father's mercy is most intense. The darkest moment in Christ's life was the very moment that He saved us, the very moment his work was done, when he cried out: "My God, my God, why have you forsaken me?" When God the Father sees anyone in the throes of that emptiness and God forsakenness because of the sinful lifestyle he has chosen for himself, God looks upon this man or woman with rose colored glasses, for He sees His Son in the throes of that emptiness, offering himself for this person.

This life is all about knowing that love, learning to allow ourselves to be loved like that, to taste that love, to receive it into ourselves. It's all about knowing the divine mercy, the pillar of fire which is the cross burning with love for us. The cross is that "pillar of fire" that banished the darkness of sin, and the Easter candle is the symbol of that pillar; the

fire that burns is Christ's love for us, and He loves us
because He loves the Father perfectly and infinitely, and so
he loves whatever belongs to the Father, especially the
individual human person, who is in the image of God.

We are caught in the middle of that love between the
Father and the Son, and when we open ourselves to that
love, our life is never the same. It is not the same because
fear is gone, and when we are touched by that love, we
want nothing else than to communicate it. To communicate
that love is like communicating a flame. If you recall the
Easter Vigil, when we lit our candles from the Easter
candle, that one little flame is shared without diminishing.
Within a minute, hundreds of little flames are burning
throughout the Church, and this one little flame from the
Easter candle is not diminished even slightly.

Clearly, this is not a zero sum process. The point is joy
is like that. When you and I have come to experience that
love, that mercy, we are not the same anymore. Our lives
are no longer governed by fear and disordered desire for
more; they are no longer governed by the anxiety that seeks
to preserve what we have. That's because our life is no
longer about pleasure, but joy. Pleasure is a zero sum
process: if there is a chocolate cake on the table for us to
share, the more I get, the less you get. But joy is not like
that, because joy is immaterial. As I share that joy by
communicating that love, by being on fire with that divine
love and allowing that fire to ignite the lives of others
around me, that joy is not diminished, but in fact becomes
greater.

The most important thing is to taste that love. When
that happens, our anxiety begins to decrease, and then we
can commit, then we can let go of sinful patterns of
behaviour, the need to control, the need to be the center of
attention, the need to be acknowledged and thanked, the
need to be loved and appreciated, the need to have a hand
in everything, the need to be consulted, the need to correct

others, the need for pleasure and ease, the need to have things work out exactly the way we want them to work out, the need to limit and control the outcomes of things, etc. In marriage, this will mean a greater openness to life. If young couples know this joy, then children make sense. But children do not make sense in a world in which pleasure is confused with joy. If we follow media coverage of anything having to do with the election or visit of a Pope, we see how preoccupied the media are with issues of sexual morality, and the reason for this inordinate preoccupation with issues surrounding sexuality is that the world does not know the joy of God's mercy; the only thing it knows is pleasure, and pleasure is a zero sum process. If all we live for is pleasure and if all we know is pleasure, then things like abortion and sexual license make perfect sense, and a morality that questions these makes no sense at all. And that's why the Church makes no sense for the western media.

Our culture is a culture of fear, and that's why it is a culture of death; and a culture of death is one of darkness. But we have to live in this culture as a people of hope, as a joyful people, as a burning flame that gives light. We have to have that light, we have to know that love, and so we have to think about it a lot, pray a lot, think about Christ, meditate on his passion, allow him to speak to us in Scripture, thus allowing him into our lives so that we can see him in our lives, arranging everything so that it works out, allowing him to show us just how happy he wants to make each one of us, individually.

18. Love and the Levels of Happiness

The other day I was thinking about how poor my memory has become. I began to notice my deteriorating memory in my early 40s, and it has only gotten worse and it will continue to do so. I used to have a very good memory as well as a great sense of direction. Not so much anymore. I tell my students that it will be their turn in due time; from the age of 21 onwards, we lose 10,000 irreplaceable brain cells every day. By the time you are 40, you begin to experience the effects. A friend of mine, however, has put a positive spin on this; he says it makes life much simpler. Of course, that is true.

But think back to last year. How much do we really remember? I can recall the last time that I was here in this Church, but I don't remember what I said, I don't remember the readings, I don't recall specific details, only vague generalities. One thing I do recall more vividly is the time when Pope Francis was elected to office. We had Mass here in the evening with a few of you, and I did the first reading without any shoes on, just my socks. I do recall it was a joyful and peaceful time. But, I have to say that even the most joyful moments in the past have less reality than a real puff of smoke in the here and now.

So we have to wonder: why live for future moments of this world, when the future will enter into the present, and will soon recede into the past, to vanish like smoke? Our gradually failing memory should make us realize that it is irrational to live for the goods and joys of this world. We should not be living for moments that will recede into the past, no matter how intensely enjoyable those moments are, but we should be living for a moment that will last forever, that will be eternal. Eternal life is an eternal moment, it is a present that endures but does not recede into the past.

This life is about preparing for that moment. And we prepare for that moment not by seeking our own happiness, but learning to concern ourselves with the happiness of others. When the Lord says be perfect as your heavenly Father is perfect, he means perfect charity (agape).

There are four Greek words for love: *eros, storge, philia,* and *agape*. *Eros* is the passionate attraction between the sexes, or romantic love, the experience of falling in love. *Storge* is a feeling of affection. *Philia* is friendship love, but *agape* is the word that Jesus uses when he commands us to love. *Agape* is the love of another, willing and seeking his good, not for what he does for us, but for his sake.

We naturally love ourselves and will the best for ourselves; we don't naturally love others, that is, we don't naturally will the best for them. That is something we have to choose to do, to will the best for the other just as we will the best for ourselves. *Agape* means loving the other as if he were another me. That's what we are commanded to do. And the reason is very simple: there is no happiness without it. The problem with this world is that people love themselves too much; people are far too preoccupied with their own happiness, and that is why happiness evades them.

The ancient Hindus and Greeks understood that there are different kinds or levels of happiness. There is 1) the happiness that comes from the experience of physical pleasure, like the happiness you experience when you are enjoying a good meal. It is a real happiness, it is good, but it is the lowest. Then there is 2) the happiness one experiences through a sense of achievement. This has been called the happiness of comparative advantage: i.e., the happiness of winning a gold medal, the happiness we experience after getting a great mark on an exam, or taking pride in an accomplishment of some kind.

A higher level of happiness is 3) natural beatitude. This involves seeing the good in others and actually doing good for them. The two previous levels of happiness are rooted in a love of self; this one, however, is rooted in a genuine love of the other, for the other's sake (agape). It is not the highest level, but it is a level that few seem to reach. When we finally decide to make the happiness of others our main focus in life, it is only then that we will discover the happiness we have always been looking for.

The highest level of happiness is called 4) sublime or supernatural beatitude. This is so lofty that it cannot be described; it involves a losing of oneself in the supernatural love of God. It is mystical, and only God can elevate us to this level.

Happiness is something that evades most people, and the reason is that human beings insist on level 1 and/or 2 happiness; levels 3 and 4 are often neglected. In fact, many think level 3 is for the government: "Let the government take care of the needs of others while I pursue my dreams". It's very hard to free ourselves from the clutches of levels 1 and 2 and to place ourselves habitually in level 3, because the happiness of level 3 is the result of choosing to live a life governed by agape.

To live in *apage* is to live an expanded existence; for I choose to love others as another me, as another self, and so I become more than what I without ceasing to be what I am. The more people I love like that, the larger I become, and the happier I become, for the happiness of the other has become my own. That is why heaven is unimaginably joyful; the happiness of the blessed is also our own happiness, not to mention the happiness of God. This happiness is an ecstasy, an exit of self or a complete loss of self in the supernatural charity of God. Those who have chosen to love only themselves cannot understand this, because they just don't know the joy of an expanded existence; all they know is the happiness of level 1 and 2. But everyone wants the highest level of happiness, it is just that many people are their own worst enemies and they will not permit themselves to achieve it; for they have chosen to make themselves the center of their universe.

We often hear people say: "I wish this moment could last forever". It is a wish that can come true, because eternity is an eternal moment that will never recede into the distant past. To those who have never loved, that moment will be an eternal torment and shame; to those who are committed to self-expansion through love, it will be an eternal and inconceivable joy.

19. Marriage and the Touch of Christ

Although today is Marriage Sunday, the readings do not directly bear upon marriage, only indirectly. Jesus touches a leper who has great faith: "If you choose, you can make me clean". Jesus moved with compassion replies: "I do choose. Be made clean".

As I said earlier, it is the touch of Christ that heals. And that is why he became flesh, to be able to touch us with his own flesh and blood, and every time we receive him in the Eucharist, he touches us with his own flesh and blood. The Eucharist heals, just like good food heals over time.

Sometimes I will flip through the TV channels and will come across the Daily Mass, recorded at St. Basil's Church in Toronto, and whenever they turn the camera to the congregation, I think to myself: 'How sad'. The Church is empty, except for about 5 or 6 people who obviously get it. There is so much suffering in this world, physical, mental, emotional, marital, work related, etc., and Christ alone heals, because he is God, the Second Person of the Trinity, the eternal Word, our origin and end, and he touches us literally, in the flesh, in this Eucharistic mystery, and out of all the people who need healing in that area of the city, about 5 or 6 are there ready to receive his touch. And that might be an accurate reflection of every city. Why is there so much brokenness in the world if such healing is available? The answer, I believe, is that there is so little faith, which is precisely why Jesus said he could only work a few signs (miracles) in his home town of Nazareth.

And Christ alone heals marriages, because Christ is the Bridegroom, and he came among us to take a Bride to himself. I used to have a poster in my classroom that said "Christ is the third party of every marriage". If he isn't, the couple will very likely experience serious trouble not too long after the initial ceremony.

There are some good signs today among young people, at least the ones I currently have in my classroom. Although the majority of people in Scandinavian countries are not getting married, but cohabitating, the vast majority of young people I encounter want to be married. But I always challenge my students to tell me what it is that they want when they say they want marriage. What exactly does 'marriage' mean? They find the answer very difficult to articulate. And that is understandable, because they have been raised in a culture that no longer really understands what marriage is; we think it is something that Parliament can define and redefine at will. But it's fun to push young people to try to articulate what it is they really want, and eventually they begin to articulate that what they want is someone who will give not just a part of himself (or herself), but his (her) entire self to the other, and the other wants to reciprocate, that is, receive that complete and total self-giving, and give her entire self to him. That mutual self-giving, if it is a total self-giving, will have certain properties.

It is an irrevocable self-giving precisely because it is total; if I give something partially and hang on to a part of it, I can revoke that giving by pulling back. But if I give all of it without hanging on to even a part of it, I cannot retrieve it. If a couple genuinely give themselves entirely to one another, that self-giving is an irrevocable gift, for no part of them has been held back. That is why a genuine marriage is an indissoluble one flesh union. A valid marriage cannot be dissolved. The two have given one another an irrevocable identity of "spouse" which cannot be undone any more than one can undo one's identity as a parent. That's a very weighty thing, to be willing to give that.

And because marriage is a mutual and total giving of one's bodily self to another, it is till death, for only death can take my body from another or the other's body from me. So, to intend a temporary union is not to intend a marriage. And, because a couple that intends to marry intends a one flesh union, there must be an openness to children. It does not mean that a child must ensue—that's not always possible; a couple can find themselves infertile—, but that openness to life is a necessary condition for a valid marriage.

Marriage is a very noble and holy vocation, but it is a very difficult vocation, because it's about learning to love. Hence, not everyone can be married, because not everyone has the moral capacity and the psychological maturity to actually give him or herself totally and completely to another, for better or for worse, in sickness and in health, till death part them. If a man cannot make smaller sacrifices, for example, is unwilling to stop smoking pot despite his fiancé's repeated appeals, or if he refuses to give up old vices that continue to weaken the relationship, it is realistically not possible for him to give his entire self to another—I can't give the whole of me, but refuse to give a part; but I can give only a part while refusing to give the whole. And that is why many so called "marriages" within the last 40 years or so have been invalid—and why there are a lot of annulments. Many think they are ready for marriage because they are full of the excitement and the exhilaration of embarking on something new, but their love, although it is sweet as candy, is often as weak as candy and as such, it simply cannot support the difficulties that are in store for every married couple.

But if a couple's marriage is valid, then the sacramental graces are there to help them become good and faithful spouses and good parents. But every marriage needs healing, because every human life needs constant healing, and the touch of Christ alone heals. It's up to the couple to approach the Lord with the very same faith as the leper in the gospel: "If you choose, you can make me clean. You can heal us Lord". If he sees that faith in a couple struggling to love one another as Christ loves his Bride, he

will be moved with pity, stretch out his hand and touch
them, saying: "I do choose. Be made clean." But we have to
allow him to touch us; we have to have the eyes of faith to
see him literally in this sacrifice of the Mass. Our entire
married life has to be centered on the Mass, and nothing
else.

20. Lying: the Antitheses of Prayer

For a large portion of the population, including adults, lying has become second nature. Most adolescents routinely lie to get out of class, to avoid a test, etc., and many adults lie habitually because their lying has for years gone unchallenged. But Scripture reveals that lying is inconsistent with life in the Person of Christ (Cf. Mt, 5, 37; Eph 4, 17-25; Col 3, 9).

Ethics is first and foremost about character (from the Greek: *ethos*, "character"). The human person establishes his moral identity (character) by the choices that he makes. You are what you choose (intend), not what you eat. If I choose to lie, I become a liar.

A liar is a person who cannot be trusted. Moreover, the liar brings about a "split" within himself, that is, a division, a degree of disintegration. In the lie there is a separation between what is in the liar's word and what is in his mind, for although the truth is in his mind, it is not in his word. And so there is a part of himself that is not integrated into another part (his words), namely his mind that knows what is in fact true. In this sense, the liar lacks integrity, or integration.

The Son is the *Logos*, the Word of the Father, His perfect self-expression, for the Word is one in being with the Father: "the Word was with God, and the Word was God" (Jn 1, 1). There is never a separation between the Word and the Father such that the Word is no longer the perfect image and expression of the Father. But man has been created in the image and likeness of God. Hence, I am to become increasingly one with my word; it ought to be an extension and expression of myself. For the more our word becomes united and filled with the content of the truth that is in us, the more like God we become. The more our word is emptied of that content and is made to express not ourselves but some other falsehood (as happens when we lie), the more unlike God we become. When the liar brings about this split between his word and his inner self, he very gradually leads himself downward towards a state of personal disintegration, the very antithesis of holiness. Interestingly enough, lying involves a kind of meditation. Consider a poorly constructed lie: "I couldn't return your urgent call because I was out all weekend, hunting elephants." It is rather easy to see through such a lie, for not much thought went into it. But a better lie is a more carefully crafted lie, and that requires more thought and meditation.

Why meditation? The reason is that the mind thinks, but the spirit meditates, and when the liar thinks of the best way to craft his lie, his spirit is open to the best suggestions. But spirit opens upon spirit, not flesh. The spirit of the liar does not open upon God, who is Spirit and Truth, but upon the spirit whom Christ refers to as "the father of lies" (Jn 8, 44), whom Scripture refers to as the most crafty of all God's creatures (Gn 3, 1). The crafty liar engages in a kind of anti-prayer. And the discrepancy between the elements of the self that the liar brings about in choosing to lie is a fissure through which the influence of darkness seeps in even further.

As the liar continues to lie—for we are creatures of habit—, he gradually loses himself, and at some point his loss is virtually irretrievable. And he will begin to delight in his lies, because through his successes he demonstrates to himself his apparent intellectual superiority over everyone who is taken in, all of whom have become a means to his own ends, puppets within the environment he schemes to construct for himself.

Lying is the very antithesis of prayer, and its effects are equally opposed to those of genuine prayer, such as integration, light, community, and salvation. The only remedy against lying is a commitment that absolutely excludes it, always, everywhere, and in every circumstance.

21. A Note on Modesty of Apparel

If the good of a thing consists in its proper operation or function, then all we have to ask in order to begin to understand what constitutes modesty of apparel is: "What is the purpose of clothing?" What is its function? The obvious answer is to protect us from the elements. But once that is accomplished, can we adjust or modify our apparel in some way in order to serve a secondary purpose? Some students of mine will say that clothing is for the sake of self-expression. And of course that is true—who can deny it? So, what is it that a person tries to express in his choice of apparel? If we can answer that question, we are closer to solving this difficulty.

The school uniform expresses the fact that one is a student of the school. That identity, however, is temporary. The choice of clothing one would wear to a funeral expresses something in that person, i.e., his or her sense of grief. People often wear black, because black was at one time an unfashionable color. At a funeral, one does not want to appear to be concerned about fashion; we want to express that we are not interested in ourselves at this time, but that our hearts "go out to" the one who has lost a loved one and who is grieving. Wearing bright and joyful colors to a funeral would call attention to the person wearing them, and such colors do not express the feeling of grief, and so they do not express a sense of solidarity with those who have lost a loved one. So it can be argued rather convincingly that the "wrong" apparel at a funeral could manifest a lack of empathy. It fails to accurately express one's interior, or what one's interior ought to be (i.e., solidarity with the grieving).

Similarly, we dress for a party accordingly; we wouldn't wear a black suit and a serious demeanour to a party. Moreover, the reason clergy wear black is that at one time, as was said above, black was unfashionable, and clergy and religious (nuns, monks, etc.) saw dress as an expression of one's interior disposition (one's character). They chose to dress unfashionably in order to express that they are unconcerned about the goods of this world (fashion) and that their lives are directed towards eternal goods (i.e., the kingdom of God). To be joyful and at the same time to dress unfashionably is to give genuine witness that one's joy does not come from the goods of this world, that is, from looking good, but from something transcendent (i.e., higher goods).

But what about those who are not priests, monks, sisters, etc.? The moral requirement is to dress modestly. But what does that mean? What is modest for one culture or time period is immodest for another. So how do we know? This is not an easy question to answer, but I believe we can come close to determining what constitutes modest dress within a particular cultural setting by looking to the purpose of clothing. One significant purpose of dress is to express one's character, that is, who one is. Now, our fundamental moral obligation is to cultivate morally beautiful character (the *kalon*). Thus, one should dress "beautifully", that is, in a way that expresses "beautiful character". That does not necessarily mean always dressing "to the hilt". Dressing simply may be an expression of one's character; dressing professionally may also be an expression of one's character, etc.

Now, we are drawn to people of like character, and we are drawn to clothing or apparel that expresses who we are, or who we want to become. So, "Is this or that person dressing modestly?" Does this person dress himself or herself with reasonable restraint? The following questions may help to answer this question: When we look at this person, what do we see? Do we see a morally beautiful person? Or do we see too much? Does the clothing draw us towards this person *as a person*, that is, as a person of intelligence and moral beauty? Or does the apparel draw us to this person as someone who can possibly satisfy a sexual appetite (lust) within us? If you are a woman, you can ask yourself: "Does this apparel accurately express who I am?" If you are a person who wants to arouse another or others sexually, then you will dress accordingly. The problem in this case, however, is your character; you are the kind of person who would like to be reduced to an object of sexual consumption, or the kind of person who has little regard for the moral integrity of others insofar as you intend to focus their gaze on you in a way that compromises their character. It may also be indicative of a lack of due self-respect. Why? Because you are more than that; but some women are so desperate to be loved that they will go to great lengths in order to be desired and loved.

Now some women are just not aware that what they are wearing is inappropriate (unbefitting a person of morally beautiful character), because they are unaware of how their apparel is affecting others, in particular those of the opposite sex. Women are not visually stimulated, but men are. Some women are unaware of this, so they are oblivious to the effects of their revealing clothing. They might also assume that "if everyone dresses this way, it must be okay"

Moreover, some men are not attracted to women of good character, that is, women who are intelligent, prudent, shrewd, and morally beautiful, because they know that they cannot sustain their facade for long, that these women will eventually see through them and thus reject them. They are drawn to women who are not so smart, not so emotionally healthy, but needier and of lesser moral character. Such women are willing to do what it takes to be accepted; they are more open to being used. The woman who dresses in a way that appeals to that kind of man (character) is opening up a path to trouble; she is attracting to herself the wrong kind of person.

The more we think about this, the more we should see that these questions are not easy to resolve. We should avoid the two easy alternatives to difficult moral questions: the extremes of absolutism and relativism. There is an objective standard, namely reason, but its application is not fixed and unchanging like a steel ruler. It is more like the measuring tape tailors use: it bends to various situations, but the standard remains universal (15 inches is 15 inches, even though every neck is somewhat different). Some instances of women's apparel are easily identifiable as immodest, others are barely immodest and barely modest, thus very difficult to determine; other instances are safely in the modest range, and others still are without much doubt excessively modest (they hide a woman's character by making her look either ugly or funny, or strange, slightly off, when in fact she isn't strange or off).

It says a lot that at one time, no one but strippers would model a bikini. Cultural arrogance allows us to easily dismiss those of another period as sexually repressed; it is quite possible, however, that there is something wrong with us. I personally lean towards the old style swimwear for women, only because when looking at such women, they remain beautiful and personal. Many women on the typical beach these days appear desirable; very few strike me as beautiful and personal. This is not to deny that they are morally beautiful and personal; rather, their chosen apparel simply fails to reveal it.

22. Pax and Peacemaking

As I was proclaiming the gospel today on this Solemnity of Christ the King, a thought occurred to me as I read Jesus' response to Pilate: "If my kingdom did belong to this world, my attendants would be fighting to keep me from being handed over to the Jews. But as it is, my kingdom is not here."

I was about to read it again, momentarily forgetting that I was in front of a large congregation. So I left it, but was resolved to return to it later. The reason I was struck by this text is that my students were recently required to attend a full day retreat given by Christian pacifists who advocate complete and total non-violence. In their minds, not only is war never justified, students were told that should someone break into their home while they are present, they should offer no physical resistance whatsoever, but should instead talk to the criminal, appeal to his humanity, perhaps call a friend to come and join in peaceful discourse; but under no circumstances should they reach for a two by four, a knife, much less a hand gun to deter him from his criminal intent and drive him out. After proclaiming that gospel, I thought: "Jesus was no pacifist". Had the very idea of a physical battle been morally repugnant to him, he would not have said "my attendants would be fighting to keep me from being handed over to the Jews"; it's just that there is no human way to battle against the enemy that he in fact came to defeat, namely sin and death, and the only way to defeat that enemy was the Way of the Cross.

Although I have never been a fan of violent sport, never have I had any sympathy for absolute pacifism. And after reading the New Testament repeatedly for the past 40 years or so, not once had I the impression that the teachings of Christ in any way provided the slightest support for absolute pacifists. Jesus made a whip out of chord and drove the money changers out of the temple, overturning their tables; he didn't talk to them, appealing to their humanity. He knew the human heart, which is why he likened some human beings to swine and others to dogs: "Do not give to dogs what is holy; and do not throw your pearls in front of pigs" (Mt 7, 6), and he foretold his passion and death more than once.

The seventh beatitude, which seems to be the cornerstone upon which the entire edifice of Christian pacifism is built, is "Blessed are the peacemakers; for they shall be called children of God". The Greek term 'peacemaker' is derived from *eiro*, which means to join or tie together into a whole. The Latin *pax* has the same meaning, which is 'unity'. A person who disturbs the peace is one who divides.

Most of us misunderstand the meaning of *pax* in that we associate it with an absence of conflict; its more direct and positive meaning is 'unity'. A virus is a threat to an organism's unity or physical integrity, which is why a very complex biochemical army goes to work to eradicate the virus. Our immune system is a peacemaker, for it preserves the integrity, the unity or *pax* of the organism. The state of peace as absence of conflict is the result of the work of the immune system, which is a work of conflict, a battle. Without that biochemical army, there is no peace, whether that is taken to mean integrity (unity), or whether it is taken as a state characterized by an absence of conflict.

Similarly, every nation and city has its own immune system, which is its military and police force respectively. Without them, there is no *pax,* that is, no peace.

There is nothing intrinsically wrong with repelling an aggressor with sufficient force, that is, a force that is proportionate to the aggression—a tank is not repelled by a shotgun. Killing only becomes homicide when the act is accompanied by a contra-life will, and homicide is never justified. But the death of the aggressor can also be *praeter intentionem*, that is, outside the intention of the agent, as it is in legitimate self-defence cases. My intention is to stop the aggressor, and if the only way to stop him from harming my family is to hit him over the head with a two by four— or perhaps to use a gun—, there is nothing intrinsically wrong with doing so, even if the action results in the aggressor's death.

Jesus was no pacifist, much less was he a political activist driven by an unscrupulous optimism; he is, rather— at least according to the faith of the Church—, the Saviour, and eternal Person of the Son, the Second Person of the Trinity, who joined a human nature in order to defeat an enemy that man had no power to defeat: "It was to undo all that the devil has done that the Son of God appeared" (1 Jn 3, 8). The parables in the synoptic gospels are not dreams of an ideal state; they are parables of the kingdom of God, a kingdom not of this world. For if a utopia was what Jesus came to establish, then his followers would be fighting. But they are not fighting, not because self-defence is a bad thing—Peter carried a sword (Mt 26, 51-53)—, but rather because Jesus had come to conquer an invisible enemy, a kingdom of darkness, the debt of sin, and its wages, which is death: "Now sentence is being passed on this world; now the prince of this world is to be overthrown. And when I am lifted up from the earth, I shall draw all men to myself" (Jn 12, 31-32).

23. Purity of Heart

When I was looking over the readings for this Sunday, I was trying to find a common thread; usually the readings have a common theme. Sometimes it is hard to find, but after a few minutes, I can usually see it. The common theme for these readings was, I found, very difficult to discover.

In the first reading, Samuel is called by God, but he thinks it was Eli who is calling him. Finally, Eli tells him that the next time you hear that voice calling, say "Speak, Lord, you servant is listening." The second reading is about fornication; sexual immorality. Finally, the gospel relates John the Baptist pointing to the Lamb of God. It is the second reading about fornication that is making it difficult to find the common thread. What does the first reading and the gospel have to do with sex?

I might have figured it out, however; perhaps it is this: Eli is the high priest of Shiloh. The name Eli means "God on high". He is training the young Samuel, who is unable to discern that the call he hears is from God, and not from Eli. The next time you are called, reply "Speak, Lord, your servant is listening".

Eli taught Samuel to listen, to maintain a posture of silent and patient openness to the voice of God. That implies an active turning to God, and as the name Eli suggests, a looking upward, on high, to the Lord who is on high. The second reading suddenly addresses sexual immorality. The reason is that the passions affect our ability to look upward, that is, they affect our ability to maintain a posture of silent and patient openness to God. To illustrate this, I will share with you something I have discovered over the years about my students.

I teach the Theory of Knowledge course for the International Baccalaureate program at our school, which is a worldwide program for high school students. I teach grade 12s, but I also teach the IB grade 9 students—we call them pre-IB. The grade 9 pre-IB students are a very interesting bunch; they are an interesting blend of intelligence and innocence. Many of them are still children, but they can exhibit extraordinary insight into the loftiest subjects. They are very interested in the most abstract ideas, such as the relationship between eternity and time, whether we can prove the existence of God by the concept of God alone, how to prove the immortality of the soul, some are interested in quantum mechanics and particle physics at such a young age, etc. There's a quality about many of them that is almost angelic— innocence and extraordinary brilliance. With some of them, it's even hard to imagine that they've ever sinned.

But what I find particularly interesting is that when I teach a lesson or two on sexual morality, the grade 9s become very quiet. They stop asking questions; they are uncomfortable. They don't get why we're talking about this and would like to just move on to what they see as more interesting subjects for discussion, such as whether we will be subject to time in heaven, or whether the happiness of the beatific vision will be enough, whether angels are subject to time and place, etc. It's quite amusing to witness this.

The senior students, on the other hand, are very much interested in sexual ethics and have lots of questions, and they are not as interested in the loftier and more abstract subjects, much less the mystical. While the younger students like to discuss metaphysical issues, the older students like to discuss physical issues. I can get into some very lofty discussions with my grade 9s, discussions about spirituality, mysticism, and prayer that I cannot get into with my grade 12s. A lot of this has to do with the fact that the grade 12s are not as innocent as the grade 9s, they are less pure in heart than the younger ones.

If you notice that Beatitude: blessed are the pure in heart, the final part of that beatitude is: and they shall see God. It is the only Beatitude that ends with: "and they shall see God". The others are: the kingdom of heaven belongs to them, or they shall be satisfied, or they will inherit the earth, etc. But the pure in heart will see God. Not only that, but that seeing begins now. The pure of heart acquire a sense of God in their lives, an understanding of God, for they experience His presence, and they acquire a wisdom that is beyond their years.

St. Thomas Aquinas wrote that the offspring of lust include a loss of interest in things spiritual, and a dulling of the mind. Lust, of course, is not sexual desire, but disordered sexual desire. There's a difference. Lust is loving another for what that person can do for you sexually. The result, Aquinas points out, is a loss of interest in things spiritual and a dulling of the mind.

In other words, there's a real link between this over-sexualized culture of ours, and its lack of interest in things spiritual and philosophical. My students have noticed this when they read international newspapers. Many of the papers around the world report on very different matters and show different cultural interests. In North America, they see that there is a great preoccupation with celebrities, with gossip, the body, with looking good, with pleasure, and sexual scandals, mixed in with a bit of important news, but in many of the countries in Asia and the Middle East, there is a greater interest in the struggle for justice, religion, truth, and far less interest in trivial matters.

The Church teaches the importance of chastity, of honouring the sexual act as an act of marriage, not because the Church wants to limit the amount of fun that we can have, but because the Church has always seen that sexual immorality affects how we see reality, especially how we see ourselves in relation to God. The body is good, and it is the temple of the Holy Spirit, as we read in the second reading, and so what we do with our body has a direct bearing on whether or not our body becomes a suitable dwelling for the Holy Spirit.

What we allow our eyes to see and our ears to hear deeply affects our relationship with God and others. Pornography, for example, is highly addictive, and it actually alters the chemistry of the brain, according to neurosurgeon, Dr. Donald Hilton. It causes an erosion of the cells of the frontal lobe of the brain, the executive function of the brain, the brake pads, so to speak, and ongoing exposure to highly provocative images of a sexual nature causes the dopamine to over stimulate the cells of the frontal lobe, wearing them out, as brake pads get worn, and the result is that a person becomes far more impulsive and less able to control those impulses, unable to stop the car, so to speak. And of course his mind is so immersed in the realm of the body and pleasure that he loses interest in and lacks insight into things spiritual.

In the gospel, John the Baptist, who lived an austere life of a prophet, living in the desert, eating locusts and wild honey, is clear sighted. He recognizes what no one else recognizes. At the beginning of the gospel of John, it is written that the Word through whom all things came into existence was in the world, and the world did not recognize him. But John the Baptist does. He says: Behold, the Lamb of God. And John's two disciples begin to follow Jesus. John's work is done: Jesus said that among those born of woman, not one is greater than John the Baptist. And yet the meaning of John's entire life is to be nothing more than a clear sign, a pointer, to Christ.

That's what it means to be a complete human person. The meaning of our existence is to be a sign pointing away from ourselves towards Christ, so that others leave us behind in order to cleave to Christ.

That's why making acts of personal sacrifice and working to cultivate the virtues, especially the virtue of chastity, is so important. That's going to be the message in the readings as we approach Lent, in preparation for Holy Week, and the good news of the resurrection.

24. The Basic Figure of Love

Whenever I hear this first reading from Ezekiel, I think of the role of the bishops of the Church. Bishops and their priests have a tremendous responsibility to warn the people. Certainly all of us have a grave responsibility to warn those in our lives who are choosing a life of sin; the first reading makes that clear, but Bishops and priests have a special responsibility. Bishops are shepherds, and their vocation is to watch out for wolves and carefully watch that the sheep are not lead astray. The Lord says to Ezekiel: "You I have appointed watchman for the house of Israel; when you hear me say anything, you shall warn them for me. If I tell the wicked, "O wicked one, you shall surely die," and you do not speak out to dissuade the wicked from his way, the wicked shall die for his guilt, but I will hold you responsible for his death". That's a serious warning to us.

Within the last 40 years, I think we've witnessed, in many parts of the Church throughout the world, a great deal of silence on the difficult parts of the gospel in particular, a silence often rationalized behind a veil of compassion. There's a lot of institutionalized evil in this culture, but we don't often hear it pointed out from the pulpits, for we don't take too kindly to prophets who very clearly and definitively give warning. In the second reading, Paul says: "Brothers and sisters: "Owe nothing to anyone, except to love one another; for the one who loves another has fulfilled the law. The commandments, 'You shall not commit adultery; you shall not kill; you shall not steal; you shall not covet,' and whatever other commandment there may be, are summed up in this saying, namely, 'You shall love your neighbor as yourself.' Love does no evil to the neighbor; hence, love is the fulfillment of the law."

This is such an important reading, because our culture has done a rather thorough job confusing so many of us about what it means to love. Everyone agrees that we should love one another, but few people seem to understand the concrete implications of love. What does love mean? Paul's letter provides a few boundaries: "You shall not commit adultery; you shall not kill, you shall not steal, you shall not covet, and whatever other commandment there may be,..." these are all summed up in the one saying: "You shall love your neighbour as yourself". It is significant that Paul begins his outline with a sexual matter. That's obviously something people needed to have clarified for them right from the beginning. Adultery is inconsistent with love. To engage in the sex act outside of marriage is not loving; it is selfish, and selfishness is not consistent with love of neighbour.

Marriage is a complete and mutual giving of the self to one another until death severs that union. To commit oneself to another until death, to promise to remain faithful to that total self-giving, especially during difficult times— and there are many difficult periods in a marriage—, requires a rather heroic ability to love—which is why most marriages today are failing. Because marriage is a one flesh union, it is consummated and expressed in the act of sexual union, in which the two actually become one body sexually, thus becoming reproductively one organism. If that act is not to be an outright lie, it must be the embodiment of a love that is undivided, and thus exclusive, and total, that is, until death. In short, a wedded love.

But contemporary culture has been so influenced by the Individualism and Hedonism of the 1960's that it no longer understands what marriage is, much less the meaning of the sexual act. Most people today think this life is about enjoyment; we're here to enjoy ourselves, to feel good, and if you believe marriage will make you feel good, get married—at least until it "gets old". If you don't think it will maximize your enjoyment, then don't get married. If a sexual relationship is what you want, without all the demands of a marital commitment, then that's your right. If you get pregnant and a baby is going to impede your ability to get the most out of life, then you have the right to have an abortion—after all, this life is about experiencing the maximum amount of enjoyment within the short time we are given. Sex in this culture has no other meaning than personal enjoyment, and marriage is regarded by many as an unnecessary restriction on this particular activity.

People are not, generally speaking, horrified by the destruction of unborn human life, and the Church's teaching against contraception makes about as much sense to most people of this culture as forbidding the taking of aspirin—although this issue is a great deal more subtle than other moral issues, to be sure. Euthanasia is becoming increasingly acceptable, all because life is about enjoyment—and sickness is not enjoyable. Television has been lewd for decades now, but it is increasingly pornographic; censorship seems to be limited not so much to eliminating foul language—which is ever increasing—, but to bleeping it.

There's a reason Paul was inspired to begin with a commandment bearing upon the sexual. Sexual pleasure is particularly vehement for a reason: the survival of the species depends on it. But it is because of its vehemence that we need to take extra measures to control it. For the greatest enemy of supernatural charity is the inordinate love of self, and we carry the wounds of Original Sin, one of which is concupiscence, which is an inordinate desire for physical gratification. It is so easy to love another human being for what he or she does for me, and it is very difficult to love another person for his or her own sake. But this is precisely what we are called to in order to prepare for heaven: to love God for His sake, not for His gifts, and to love our neighbour for his or her sake alone, not for our sake. It takes a lifetime with many trials to cultivate the virtues necessary to achieve this, but we must achieve it, because the self-centered would be very uncomfortable in heaven among the communion of saints.

Without even realizing it, we often do love others for what they do for us, but the commandments are really the boundaries that clearly outline the basic figure of love of others. Without that outline, love will mean whatever we want it to mean, and it will no longer be possible to distinguish love from selfishness, which is the situation we find ourselves in today with respect to popular culture.

Notice that the first three commandments have to do with our relationship to God: Have no other gods before me (i.e., the god of self, or money, or power, or pleasure), do not take the Lord's name in vain, but revere it and live to glorify it; Keep holy the Sabbath day (get to Mass every single Sunday and feed on the Bread of Life). These, especially the latter, are commandments, not recommendations nor invitations that one is free to turn down as if one could have more important things to do.

The next seven commandments, however, have to do with our neighbour. They come after because we simply cannot love our neighbour authentically unless we love God first. If we don't love God first, we will love our neighbour for our sake, on the basis of what he or she does for us.

The first of the seven deals with our parents: honour them, forgive them, and do not hold resentment towards them. The next has to do with reverence for human life: every individual human person exists in the image and likeness of God and has an immeasurable value. To destroy human life in order that our lives may be easier is completely antithetical to everything Christ is. To remain indifferent to the plight of the starving in our world, to contribute to creating the conditions that cause poverty by indifference to the poor is to live in the darkness of sin. And if we revere human life, we will respect another's right to own property; we won't take what rightfully belongs to someone else, no matter how small it is—we won't take the sale sticker and place it on an item that is not on sale, and we'll let the cashier know when he or she has given us too much change. We won't allow ourselves to be tainted by envy. If we truly love our neighbour, we won't gossip, nor delight in the misfortunes of others. The pure of heart do not delight to hear bad news.

Because this culture cannot tolerate the sight of its own depravity, it has invented a new morality, enshrined in a cultural orthodoxy to which everyone is expected to remain faithful and obedient. Moral permissiveness, especially in sexual matters, now becomes disguised as tolerance for diversity; concern for the environment is a good thing in itself, but it has become so accentuated that our achievements in this area have allowed us to feel righteous. The New Age has become the new religion, and this is a religion without the demands of personal reform; it is a religion geared towards personal financial success and physical health; a religion of the self. A great deal of immorality is allowed to continue under the cover of cleanliness. It should remind us of what Jesus said to the Pharisees: "You are whitewashed tombs full of the bones of dead men". Corruption under the guise of cleanliness and respectability.

The Lord calls us out of this deception. He calls us to true freedom, to joy, to holiness, to die to self. The responsorial psalm says: "If today you hear God's voice, harden not your hearts." Why? Because today might be the only day He allows you the extraordinary grace to hear His voice—for He does not owe us graced moments. His calling us out of darkness into His light is sheer gift, entirely gratuitous. And if He chooses today to call you from within the depths of your conscience, it is a dangerous thing to harden your heart in a spirit of pride, because that might be your only window.

This life is not about enjoyment or pleasure; it is about joy; this life is about preparing for the eternal banquet that the king will give in honor of his Son, Jesus Christ, the complete figure of love. And we prepare by growing in moral integrity, by cultivating the virtues, especially the unpopular virtues, like chastity, temperance with respect to food, drink, rest, entertainment, the desire for new and exhilarating experiences, etc., in order to cultivate the various parts of justice, such as generosity, caring for the sick and the suffering, thoughtfulness, gratitude, religion, love of parents and country, devotion to the common good, etc. If we hear Him calling, it is a gift, and we should respond not in anger, but in a spirit of gratitude.

25. The Courage to Speak Out

I'd like to begin by commenting on the first reading. It is such a great reading when read in its full context. I'd like to give you a bit of that context. One evening King David took a stroll on the palace roof and caught site of a woman bathing. Instead of turning away, he watched her. That was his first mistake. Then he makes inquiries about her; they tell him who she was, that she had a husband, but he sent for her anyways, slept with her and she conceived a child from that encounter. That is why exercising "custody of the eyes" is so important.

What happens next is that the prophet Nathan is sent to David and asks him to judge a parable:

> "Judge this case for me! In a certain town there were two men, one rich, the other poor. The rich man had flocks and herds in great numbers. But the poor man had nothing at all except one little ewe lamb that he had bought. He nourished her, and she grew up with him and his children. She shared the little food he had and drank from his cup and slept in his bosom. She was like a daughter to him. Now, the rich man received a visitor, but he would not take from his own flocks and herds to prepare a meal for the wayfarer who had come to him. Instead he took the poor man's lamb and made a meal of it for his visitor."

David grew very angry with that man and said to Nathan: "As the Lord lives, the man who has done this merits death! He shall restore the ewe lamb fourfold because he has done this and has had no pity."

Then Nathan said to David: "You are the man! Thus says the Lord God of Israel: 'I anointed you king of Israel. I rescued you from the hand of Saul. I gave you your lord's house and your lord's wives for your own. I gave you the house of Israel and of Judah. And if this were not enough, I could count up for you still more. Why have you spurned the Lord and done evil in his sight? You have cut down Uriah the Hittite with the sword; you took his wife as your own, and him you killed with the sword of the Ammonites.

Now, therefore, the sword shall never depart from your house, because you have despised me and have taken the wife of Uriah to be your wife.'

Thus says the Lord: 'I will bring evil upon you out of your own house. I will take your wives while you live to see it, and will give them to your neighbor. He shall lie with your wives in broad daylight.

You have done this deed in secret, but I will bring it about in the presence of all Israel, and with the sun looking down.'"

Then David said to Nathan, "I have sinned against the Lord." (2 Sam 12, 1-13)

There are a number of things that I find striking about this reading. The first thing is the incredible courage of the prophet Nathan. Where do we find courage like that today? Certainly not in me. Nathan must have been afraid for his life. But the Lord commanded him to speak the truth to David, to shine the light on his vices. What a difficult thing to do, but what a loving thing to do. Because had Nathan allowed himself to be overcome by his fear, had he loved his own life more than he loved David's soul, he wouldn't have said a thing. He would have shut right up and perhaps rationalized his silence by an appeal to tolerance, patience and the principle of gradualism, and the result would have been that David would not have repented, and he would have died in his sin. But Nathan loved the Lord and loved truth and loved justice more than he loved himself.

There are not many people today in the world who love like that; hence, there are not many prophets. The kind of prophets we have today are safe prophets, those who speak out on issues that are in vogue, so that there's no chance they'll face persecution. This is why I love Archbishop Oscar Romero so much. He was the voice of the poor in his country, and he spoke out against the injustices all around him, and when reading his homilies, nothing is more obvious than that he is a bishop of the Church, first and foremost. His words are not inspired by Marxist ideology or socialism; they are rooted in the gospel as interpreted by the Church.

But he has become a caricature of the Left in North America, and that's unfortunate, because Romero always said that preaching must bear upon the sins of the nation in which one finds oneself, and the sins today in this country are not starvation wages and poor working conditions and murderous death squads hired to kill street kids, etc. The sins of today in this country are more on the personal level: fornication, infidelity in marriage, internet pornography, theft, pirating DVDs, abortion, contraception, a general indifference to injustice, and surrendering to individualism and a hedonism that sees human existence as primarily about enjoyment and pleasure, rather than living first and foremost for the kingdom of God. To emulate Romero is to preach on these things, which is just what many here refuse to do.

And this brings me to my next point about the first reading. How did David get to that point? He was a person of such tremendous character. Saul was out to kill him, and he had a chance to kill Saul, but he refused to do so and the reason was this: "No one who lifts a hand against the Lord's anointed will go unpunished" (1 Sam 26, 9). What reverence he shows for Saul's kingship. So how did he get to this point? I think the answer is this: As a result of the tendency within each of us to inordinate self-love, prosperity breeds the worst in us. We are at our worst in times of prosperity, and we are at our best in times of suffering.

I remember studying the history of the 20th century and being struck by just this point. During times of great prosperity in the 20th century, we were at our moral worst; prosperity bred a desire for more, and avarice breeds fear of loss, which in turn generates tremendous bigotry and racism, and then you have World War I, followed by a period of prosperity, which breeds moral depravity, then that is followed by the Great Depression and that brings out the best in some people. Then there is a period of prosperity, which if I remember correctly bred more depravity. But that is followed by WWII, and then prosperity after that, which was followed by the invention of the birth control pill, which is followed by the sexual revolution and the swinging 70s, the decline in marriage, the legalization of abortion, the practice of infanticide, the legalization of euthanasia, and so on.

The history of Israel is like that as well. During times of prosperity, the kings of Israel compromise with the world and Israel begins to worship other gods, false gods. That is soon followed by tragedy and suffering, which leads them to repentance. Then prosperity follows that, and the kings begin to worship false gods, all for the sake of getting along with other nations. You could say they are becoming "inclusive" and selling their principles in the process, forgetting the covenant. And then the divine hand comes upon them, the Kingdom of Israel falls to the Babylonians, and they repent.

It seems that David was enjoying great prosperity and was not careful about that propensity to sin that we inherit from the first parents of the human race. But that's why Jesus says that it is difficult for a rich man to enter the kingdom of heaven; for they live in prosperity, and in that condition it is very difficult not to make one's own enjoyment, one's own self, the center of one's life. Suffering inclines us to cry out to God, to reach out to him; it puts us in touch with our own frailty, our own radical need for God. And that's why the first Beatitude is "Blessed are those who are poor in spirit, the kingdom of heaven is theirs". To be poor in spirit is to be aware of your radical need for God.

But the third point I'd like to make about David is his whole hearted repentance. He saw his depravity, thanks to Nathan's tremendous courage and his brilliance in relating it to him using a parable, and he repented whole heartedly, which is why the Lord forgave him. He experienced tremendous sorrow for his sin and acknowledged it. He does not kill Nathan, nor does he even consider killing him; there is not a word about any kind of anger towards him. And that's a sign of great character. He is a humble and repentant king.

The Lord is merciful and forgives him. But, one thing to notice here is that God's mercy does not violate his justice. That's the problem with our mercy and justice: our justice is often without mercy, and our mercy is often unjust, for it is often nothing more than leniency, which is not a virtue. What is so marvelous about our God is that His justice is never without mercy, and his mercy is never unjust. David is forgiven, but he will have to pay for his sin. Justice is not revenge, as many of us like to think it is. Justice is a great good, and if God is Goodness Itself, God is Justice. His mercy will never violate His justice.

I've notice that so often in my work as a Deacon: God's mercy is infinite, it is marvelous to behold, but people still have to live with the consequences of their sin. God does not undo the brain damage that resulted from drug use or reverse the emotional retardation that was the result of using marijuana. They still live with that, but the Lord is there to help them through it. In fact, the Lord joined a human nature in order to suffer with us, so that we may find him in the midst of our suffering and be strengthened by his presence in the depths of our darkness.

Let us pray for the grace to emulate David's courage and character in repenting wholeheartedly from whatever sins we are aware of, and Nathan's courage in boldly proclaiming the truth that the world does not want to hear.

26. The Glory of Humility

I've always been fascinated by the sluggishness of the human mind. The brightest human beings are really quite slow. "Brightness" and "speed" are relative terms. A thing is fast only in relation to something else; a light might be bright, but once again, only relative to something else. There are bright people in this world who are quick thinkers, but only in relation to those around them who are not so bright.

I always get a sense of the slowness of my own mind when I listen to Jewish comedian, Jackie Mason. I just can't keep up with him; he's too fast for me. And his audience is obviously quicker than I am, because they're laughing. And he is genuinely funny, but I need to slow it down and think about what he's saying before I can laugh.

I often tell my students that what they learn in the course of a semester, in their math class, for example, or in their chemistry or physics classes, etc., took centuries for the most brilliant human beings to uncover. Once it has been uncovered, however, it appears to be so simple. Why did it take so long? This is true especially for philosophy. It takes years and years to dispose the intellect to learn such abstract truths, and from these truths it is possible to go on to demonstrate, through reason alone, the existence of God, and it is also possible, through reason alone, to show that God is one, eternal, the source of all that is good and beautiful, that He is Beauty Itself, Goodness Itself, and Truth Itself. And when we finally come to see it, we inevitably think: "This is so clear and simple; why did it take years to get this?"

The reason is that human beings, by nature, are slow. We are the highest beings on the hierarchy of material beings, but we are the lowest beings on the hierarchy of God's intellectual creatures. Below us are the animals, and below them are plants, etc., but above us are angels, who are immaterial creatures, and their knowledge does not depend on sensation, imagination, nor is it subject to the passing of time, because they are not physical and do not exist in time. Their knowledge is not encumbered by matter as is ours. They see at a glance what it takes centuries for human beings to learn.

The word 'human' comes from the Latin '*humus*', which means 'dirt' or 'soil'. Man is from the earth. He is made of matter; he is a spirit and matter unity. As spirit, we can think and will, but as matter, we are weighed down, limited, and are vulnerable to destruction.

The word 'humility' is derived from the same word: "*humus*". A humble person recognizes his limits, his frailty and vulnerability to destruction. He realizes that he is, fundamentally, dirt (dust and ashes).

And so we have the misfortune of being at the bottom of the hierarchy of God's intellectual creatures. But maybe it's not a misfortune; perhaps the angels of God envy us after all. There's no doubt, the glory of man does not consist in intelligence; for anyone who glories in his intelligence is in for a rude awakening when he discovers that his brilliance is only relative—compared to the choirs of angels, he's on the lowest rung of the ladder.

So what is man's glory? The glory of man lies in 'humility'. A man who is intelligent is like the angels, but imperfectly so. But when he is humble, he is true to himself. The angels can be humble, but if we want, we can outdo them in humility. They cannot recognize that they are fundamentally dirt (soil), because they are not. We can, however.

And God became flesh, joined a human nature, to show us what it means to be man, to reveal to us our glory. The image that reveals to us our true identity is the image of the cross. Our power is in the power of the cross. And that's our glory. The angels cannot share in the sufferings of Christ, they cannot enter into the humiliation of the cross, but we can. The more we do so, the more glorious we become, paradoxically enough.

It is indeed sad to see that so many adults have missed this, especially those who rebel against God by writing books in an attempt to persuade others that God does not exist, that religion is evil, that man is the measure of moral truth, and that there is nothing higher than man, neither angels, God, nor truth itself. This is nothing more than that ancient tendency in man to ascend so as to take God's place, which originated in the sin of Lucifer, the cherubim angel who fell through pride and lured the first parents of the human race into the current of his own sin.

Our life must move in the complete opposite direction. The humbler we become, the more true to our nature we are, and the result is that the more laughter there will be in our lives; for the word humour is also derived from "humus". The humbler we are, the more we are able to laugh at ourselves, for the less seriously do we take ourselves, and the more able we are to take in the humour that's always around us. That is why among the arrogant one does not encounter a great deal of laughter—except the sardonic kind that delights in the humiliation of others. The proud take themselves very seriously, but among saintly people there really is a great deal of laughter.

27. The Sin of Pharisaism

The Pharisees were a religious group that came into being in the Hebrew religious community in the 2nd century B.C. Their objective was to practice the Mosaic Law, adhering strictly to every minor detail. They were known at the time of Christ as Pharisees, a word derived from the Aramaic word *Preesha*, which means "those who separate themselves". They were not of the priestly class, they were laymen, but they enjoyed a kind of clerical status in the sense of being very "learned" in the law.

Jesus was quite hard on the Pharisees, as was John the Baptist. What Christ condemned vehemently was the sin of their hypocrisy. The word "hypocrite" is derived from the Greek *hypokrisis*, which means "acting on the stage, or pretense". A hypocrite is an actor, that is, one who plays a role. The hypocrite does not know his true self, and so he assumes a role, a pretense. It was their pretentiousness that Christ rebuked the Pharisees for, calling them "whitewashed tombs full of dead men's bones". On the outside they looked clean and impressive, observing the details of the law, but on the inside was nothing but the rot of arrogance, envy, and a false life.

The word "Pharisaic" has come to mean precisely this kind of clericalism, if you will. Pharisaism will be with us until the end of time. The reason is that there is a secret desire in the human heart to be "set apart" from others. Human persons wish to be "outstanding" in one way or another. The Pharisee sets himself apart from others in terms of his religious and clerical status. He sees himself as learned, especially in religious matters, and so he does not associate with the lowly, sinners and tax collectors, prostitutes, in short, social odd balls.

The problem, though, is that Christ ate with sinners and tax collectors, and the Pharisees saw this. They were taken aback, because to eat with another, to share a meal, is to enter into a kind of communion with the one with whom you share a meal. For Christ to eat with sinners and tax collectors was to enter into communion with them; it was to become ritually unclean. But Christ is God the Son; he is holiness itself. And so the basic error of the Pharisees is that they misunderstood the meaning of holiness. The word "sacred" means "to be set apart". One who is holy is set apart, not in terms of social status, or clerical status, but in terms of love, or charity. The one who is holy has extraordinary charity, an exceptional or extraordinary love of God and love of neighbour.

God did not separate Himself, rather He joined a human nature; He descended. He became like one of us. That's how the divine is different. Man, because his heart is proud, desires to ascend, to stand above everyone else, however subtle that might be. God is different, set apart, in that He descends, humbles himself, takes on human flesh, is born in a stable, and dies on a cross wearing a crown of thorns. He is comfortable in the presence of rejects. And those who are genuinely holy are comfortable in the presence of the lowly, the odd balls of society. In fact, many of the saints were odd balls themselves. St. John Vianney, the patron saint of priests, was so odd that his brother priests actually petitioned their bishop not to ordain him, for he was an embarrassment in the way he looked and was thought to be unfit for the priesthood; he wasn't academically brilliant, he found learning very difficult, had a very limited knowledge of math, history, and geography, and he failed his entrance exams to the seminary. The petition that his brother priests sent out inadvertently ended up on Vianney's desk. He read it, and actually agreed with it, so he signed it. His was the last signature on the petition.

Of course he was widely loved as a priest, and during the last ten years of his life he would spend between 16 to 18 hours a day in the Confessional, and the number of pilgrims who came to see him for direction reached about 20 thousand a year. Pilgrims were moved at his "exquisite politeness", his "great kindness", his graciousness, sweetness and total lack of pretentiousness.

What makes the genuinely holy person so approachable and attractive to others is a demeanour that results from being radically in touch with his own sinfulness. Because he has chosen to engage in the struggle with his sinfulness, he knows through experience—from the heart, not merely the head—that he is not even slightly better than the lowliest of sinners. The conviction that he is no higher than his weakest brother is seen in his face, in his eyes, and in the way he carries himself.

At the funeral of Terrance Cardinal Cooke of New York there were "street bums" and taxi drivers, everyone from all walks of life, because he associated with them all, mingled with street people, carried on conversations with them, had an eye to eye relationship with everyone he met.

Archbishop Romero was another great man who was down to earth and could identify with the peasant and spoke to them with great love and intimacy, much to the dismay of his brother bishops. Mother Teresa, of course, had no problems living in the midst of the worst poverty. It is the overcoming of that need to be set apart that sets the saints apart. But they've overcome that need to be set apart precisely because they chose to engage in the struggle, that basic struggle with their own particular sinfulness. And when you engage in that struggle, then you realize that you are nothing, weak, helpless to succeed, and no better than anyone, and then you can identify with and have a comfortable relationship with the most lowly, because you see them as your equal, as another you.

But that is one thing the Pharisee cannot do. He is not comfortable with the odd balls, the social misfits, because he has not and will not engage in the struggle with his own sinfulness. It's all about externals, observing the details of the law, having right doctrine, observing all liturgical rubrics correctly, etc. And it is here that they separate themselves from others and enjoy the delirious feeling of not being like them.

This kind of Pharisaism is something we find in all areas, on the left, on the right, among liberals, conservatives, in lay people, in bishops, priests, etc., and we see it in snobbery of the wealthy. We see it in the arrogance of the learned professor who writes so as not to be understood except by his academic peers; we find it in the medical profession, and in the corporate world. Wherever there is the refusal to engage in the personal struggle with one's own sinfulness, we find people assuming a role, one that includes dressing, speaking, and holding your head a certain way, associating with a certain class of people, all for the sake of procuring the admiration of others.

But in this gospel, Christ says that it is not what goes into a man from the outside that makes him unclean, but it is from within, from the heart that evil intentions emerge: fornication, theft, murder, adultery, avarice, malice, deceit, licentiousness, envy, slander, pride and folly. Christ lists the sins of the flesh, beginning with fornication, adultery, licentiousness, which refers more generally to self-indulgence with regard to the pleasures of touch. But not everyone struggles here. And so he names avarice, which is the inordinate love of possessing (the love of money and security), he names deceit, or lying, which includes the general lie of the pretentious, who are role playing. He lists envy, which involves feeling a certain sadness at another's good or at another's excellence, and feeling a secret delight in their misfortunes—all hidden, however, under the opposite facial expressions. He names slander, which involves speaking negatively against the good reputation of another; he names folly, which is acting thoughtlessly, often impulsively, and he names pride, which is the excessive love of one's own excellence and involves the illusion of self-sufficiency.

The breadth of this list is important because what happens is that we cleverly deceive ourselves: the areas where we do not struggle are the areas we accentuate and see as principally sinful. For example, if we don't struggle with sexual temptation, we tend to see sin primarily in terms of the sexual. That way we feel that sin is out there, in others, not in me. Meanwhile, we might struggle with envy, but we don't see it, because sin is focused on the sexual. On the other hand, you have those who do struggle with sexual sins, but not avarice or anger, and so they are very liberal when it comes to sexual morality, and sin becomes principally a matter of avarice, or justice.

Christ lists all of them, from the most spiritual sins of arrogance and envy, to the most physical, such as fornication and licentiousness. Our freedom will come only after we decide to engage seriously in this struggle with our own sinfulness, because only then will we come to see the need for the divine mercy, and we will seek it, find it, taste it, and become zealous channels of that mercy wherever we go and to whomever we meet.

28. Truth, Obedience, and Humility

Definitions express the essential meaning of things, and a good definition contains two parts: a genus, which tells us what something is generally, and a specific difference, which specifies the genus, as "rational" specifies the genus "animal"; hence, the definition of man. The definition of truth is "the conformity between what is in the mind and what is (i.e., extra-mental being). Note that "conformity" is the genus. Thus, truth is a relationship, precisely because it is a certain kind of conformity.

But the definition of obedience is "the conformity between one's behaviour and a command". The definition contains the same genus, namely "conformity". To obey is to conform one's behaviour to another's command (i.e., a parent, an officer, God, etc.). The resemblance between the two definitions is worth thinking about; for it gives us insight into the relationship between virtue and one's ability to possess truth.

I recall the time I walked into the school office and witnessed the biggest trouble maker in the school yell out, with seething rage: "How dare he (the principal) tell me what to do! Nobody tells me what to do! Nobody!" It should come as no surprise that this young man had a criminal record. Disobedience is the offspring of pride. A proud man refuses to obey the command of another, because it means conforming to something other than his own will, and the proud man has made himself, his own will, the measure of what is true and good.

Now, possessing truth has something to do with obedience. The reason is that both truth and obedience possess the same genus, namely conformity, and to conform implies the willingness to be formed by something other than one's own will, something other than the self. So, if disobedience is an offspring of pride, it follows that obedience is an offspring of humility. And if truth and obedience both involve conforming oneself to something other than the self, it would seem that humility is a fundamental requirement or condition for the possession of truth. Without humility, one has no hope of ever acquiring wisdom, which is the possession of ultimate truths.

Recently I heard a priest talk on Catholicism. In response to the many questions coming from some of my colleagues, he informed us all that our last two Popes (John Paul II and Benedict XVI) failed to understand the true meaning of Vatican II—which is why they have been trying to "take the Church back to the 16th century"—, that the language of the new Roman Missal is irrelevant and out of touch, that one day women will be priests, etc. What struck me, however, was not the priest's dissent—that's par for the course with this particular society of priests—, but the number of questions my colleagues were asking him. I don't have an adversarial relationship with any of these colleagues and I had been teaching at the school for over 10 years at the time, and so I found myself wondering why, if they had so many pressing questions, they did not think to ask me to try to shed light on their difficulties, or any other priest who gave similar talks—but of a more orthodox bent—in previous years.

Jean Pierre de Caussade points out, "...our wishes and desires, even if only begun to be formed, are to God what the voice is to our fellow men. He hears them, in fact, far more clearly than men hear our voices, and it is enough for Him that we form these desires; for, as the Psalmist says He knows even the mere intention and disposition of our hearts from the first moment that they begin to turn, and to move towards Him." (Abandonment to Divine Providence, Letter VIII)

That is why we always get what we ultimately want in life; for the Lord knows our deepest desires more than we know them. The book of *Wisdom* infers as much: "Wisdom is brilliant, she never fades. By those who love her, she is readily seen, by those who seek her, she is readily found. She anticipates those who desire her by making herself known first. Whoever gets up early to seek her will have no trouble but will find her sitting at the door" (Wis 6, 12-14).

In this light, I suspect the answer to my question above, namely why it is that colleagues keep their pressing questions deep within their breast for years on end—especially when so much is available at the click of a mouse, I might add—is that they know what the answers are that I or anyone else consistent with the faith of the Church will give them, and they are not the answers they want. But after listening to a liberal dissenter for only a few minutes, it became abundantly clear to them that this man will indeed provide them with the answers they want to hear, and so they ask and complain as I have never seen them do before.

As Aristotle said, "As a person is, so does he see". A person's character not only describes the kind of person he has made himself to be by the moral choices that he has made, character determines what it is he will perceive as true, good, and beautiful. A humble soul that loves truth more than he loves himself will readily see it and possess it, for wisdom "anticipates those who desire her by making herself known first". But the person who loves himself—his own will, the goods of this world, etc.,—more than wisdom will not find her sitting at his door, because she anticipates only those who desire her, for our desires are to God what the voice is to others.

A teacher cannot help the latter; he or she can only pray that they be given the grace to willingly open themselves to the prospect of conforming to something much larger and richer than themselves, namely the splendor of wisdom. Once that desire is even barely formed within their depths, Someone within will be waiting at their door to teach them. Then they will seek, and all who seek, find.

29. Some Thoughts on Utilitarianism and the Good as Such

A young student of mine recently expressed his inability to see the sense in the absolute precept that "one must not do evil to achieve good". Returning to the scenario of a man who is given the option to push a button, which will release carbon monoxide into the home of a family of five, killing all five in the middle of the night, or not push the button, in which case thousands would be summarily executed by a brutal tyrant in retaliation for not killing those five, he could not for the life of him understand how the decision not to push the button would constitute a morally responsible choice.

The classic utilitarian would regard the natural law precept that "one must not do evil to achieve good" as indefensible and irrational, at least in some well-defined circumstances. Sacrificing five innocent people to save a larger number makes perfect rational sense, according to the utilitarian; for the principle is "the greatest happiness for the greatest number of people". We should keep in mind that for Bentham and Mill (the fathers of Utilitarianism), happiness does not mean "eternal happiness", but a natural happiness which they identified with pleasure. Thus, "a good end justifies and evil means". A good end is "the greatest happiness for the greatest number", and the evil means, in this case, is the intentional killing of the five innocent people. The honest utilitarian acknowledges that if it were a matter of killing the five innocent people in order to save his own life, then he ought not to kill the five innocents but accept death from the hand of the brutal tyrant. However, if it is a matter of killing five innocent people in order to spare the lives of more than five, let's say thousands, then the utilitarian argues that the only reasonable course of action is the killing of the five innocents.

Of course, there is a problem with calculating overall maximum benefits, in other words, predicting outcomes. Is it possible to see the long term repercussions of killing the five innocent people in order to save the thousands from extinction? Can we know that in the long run, the net result will be a "maximization of happiness" for the greatest number? Is it possible that in the long run, the net results of our decision to kill five innocent people could amount to a state of affairs in which there is greater misery for the greater number? Is there any way to know that such a state of affairs will not come about? How far do we go in considering consequences? How much time do we spend calculating? And are we not assuming that we are not subject to profound limitations in our ability to predict outcomes? It seems to me that these questions, which do not seem to have coherent answers, are enough to show that utilitarianism/consequentialism is unworkable.

Nevertheless, the initial objection remains a strong one. How does one justify not intentionally killing the five innocent people in order to spare the thousands? To be fair to the utilitarian, he or she could respond to the above doubts regarding our ability to predict outcomes by insisting that we are only responsible for what is in our control and range of vision, not for what is completely outside our range of vision, and so we have to act within the limits that constrain us. A decision has to be made, and we make the decision to kill the five innocents to save thousands, thus maximizing benefits and minimizing harms. And so how does the natural law theorist defend his decision not to kill the five innocents?

He does so because he argues that morality is not about maximizing benefits for the greatest number, but about the human person's relationship to "the good"; thus, ethics is primarily about moral character (or integrity). The utilitarian wants to know why that is significant. The following is an attempt to make this intelligible and hopefully more compelling.

I am going to argue that relationship to the entire network of human goods (i.e., human life, truth, beauty, friendship, the common good, marriage, integrity and religion) is the same as our relationship to God, who is the Supremely Good. If the decision above were only about me, the five innocent people, and the remaining thousands or millions, then it would be very difficult to convince anyone of the reasonableness of not killing the five innocents, only to watch the thousands die as a result.

The moral "ought" emerges when I become aware of a conflict between what I understand to be good for me (my private good) and the alternative, which is good regardless of whether it is good for me (lying to you might spare me some trouble, but telling the truth is good regardless of how it affects me; for I have an obligation to tell you the truth because I have an obligation to treat you in a way that respects your status as equal in dignity to me). The good *as such* transcends my private good. The utilitarian who refrains from pushing the button that kills five innocents and accepts his own death (since it is only him who will die) chooses a larger good over his own private good. But he is willing to kill five innocents to spare thousands. Indeed, he acknowledges that he is intentionally killing five innocent people whose lives are basically good, as are the lives of the thousands he chooses to spare. He knows he is "adopting a proposal that includes their deaths"; in short, he is intentionally killing them (murdering them). In doing so, he is establishing a relationship between himself and the good as such (human goods without qualification), not merely the collective good that is "the thousands of people" he spares. What is this "good as such"? Allow me to elaborate.

Aquinas argues that human beings have a natural knowledge of God, but it is not necessarily a conscious knowledge. Human beings naturally seek the causes of things; in fact, the principle of sufficient reason is the driving force behind man's scientific quest (we always seek the sufficient reasons for things). All human beings have a natural desire to know. That does not come to an end when the scientist retires, for example, and it will not come to an end until the knower comes to know the ultimate cause of all things. If there isn't an ultimate cause, a first cause, then his search is in vain. He is drawn to look for something that does not exist. But it is impossible for there not to be an ultimate cause and sufficient reason for all things; for one would have an indefinite series of conditioned realities, or an indefinite series of dependent causes, which is impossible (of course, we need to do the difficult work in demonstrating this more clearly and definitively). Thus, man naturally seeks God, even if he does not know it. As well, the human person naturally desires happiness, and every end he pursues is, ultimately, for the sake of a happiness that is 1) sufficient unto itself, 2) complete (thus an end, not a means), and 3) enduring (no one wants a happiness that comes to an end). But one cannot desire what one does not know. Thus, at some level each human person knows that there is a happiness that is sufficient unto itself, complete, and enduring—otherwise he would not desire it—an end is a final cause that attracts, pulls, draws one forward. Thus, it is a real cause.

Now the only thing that answers to that description is, once again, God, who is being itself. As pure act of existing, God is sufficient unto Himself (he is not contingent and dependent upon some prior being, for He is the first existential cause of whatever exists that is not pure being itself, but contingent); He is complete (pure act of being without potentiality), and enduring (the necessary being who cannot not exist). And since good is a property of being, being itself is goodness itself; thus, human beings desire to know and possess God, without necessarily knowing it explicitly. Some think the ultimate and unqualified good (*bonum universale*) is pleasure, some think it is wealth and power, some might identify it with the collective good of all finite beings currently on the face of the earth, etc. But none of these would qualify, because each one is really a finite good; for example, pleasure is in me, and I am a finite good, so too is the object that brings me pleasure; the same reasoning applies to power and wealth; and the collective good of all human beings is also a finite good or goods.

A free moral action involves a choice between what I understand to be good for me (my private good, or the delectable good) and the alternative, which is good in itself, regardless of whether it is a delectable good (for me). It is at this very point that the moral "ought" emerges. I ought to choose the good, not merely my own good: for the good as such, the good without qualification, is larger than my private good. The utilitarian would agree, but not when it comes to the collective good of five innocent people over the collective good of thousands of lives. The natural law position argued here is that the one individual person who refrains from killing the five innocent people (and who accepts the consequences, i.e., the obliteration of thousands) is establishing a relationship between himself and a real existing good (not merely an idea). The good as such—not merely my good—is a real existing good, which we are identifying with the supreme good, namely God Himself. The utilitarian, on the contrary, identifies the greatest good as the "greatest pleasure for the greatest number".

Thus, for natural law, every morally good action is, at some level, a religious act. I say at some level, because this is true even for the atheist who has no conscious awareness of and belief in God, and who might think God is merely a fiction. To choose not to intend evil as a means to an end, to choose the good as such by freely choosing to refrain from intentionally destroying human goods (five innocents) for the sake of other human goods (the collective good of thousands), thus allowing these thousands to perish for the sake of one's relationship to the good, is really a choice to love God over self, even if one is unconscious of the fact. But isn't that selfish, asks the utilitarian? Isn't that unreasonable? Are you not putting your relationship to the good (God Himself) above the lives of these thousands who will now die?

It is undeniable that you are putting your relationship to the good (God Himself) above the lives of the thousands, for the decision not to do evil as a means to an end is a choice to love God over everything else, including the collective good of the thousands upon thousands. So it seems we are saying that your integrity (character) and your relationship to God (religion) is a greater good than my physical existence and the physical existence of all human lives. Thus, in principle, you would not be permitted to rape and murder an innocent girl to save an entire nation, and you would not be permitted to torture a child indefinitely in order to save the world, etc.

Moreover, this decision to refrain from killing five innocents is also an act of hope in God, even though one might not be explicitly aware that it is. To place our hope in someone is to trust in him or her. Thus, if what is said here is true, then this hope in God is at the same time an act of natural faith in God—again, even if one is consciously an atheist.

But the utilitarian could ask: "What is it about God that is hoped for or believed in, given that it is unconscious?" This is a difficult question to answer. If God is unlimited, if He is Being Itself, then He has complete dominion over being (existence). Hence, He is all-powerful. Moreover, we are all too aware of our own powerlessness, not only in predicting outcomes, but in bringing about a decent state of affairs in this world (there is unspeakable poverty and injustice in this world, despite our good intentions and our attempts to overcome this). The natural law position really amounts to following our obligation to do the good that we are capable of doing and choosing not to do the evil that we are capable of doing, even for the sake of what we judge will be a better overall state of affairs in the world. Perhaps in doing so, we commend ourselves, at some level and in a spirit of unconscious hope and trust, to the providence of God. Perhaps if we begin to do so (commend ourselves, in an unconscious hope and trust, to God), this world will be the better place that we intend for it to be but have not yet been able to bring about on our own efforts. Perhaps the problem is that in doing evil to achieve good, believing that it will maximize overall benefits for the world, we are only making matters worse in the long run, because we simply cannot foresee the long term repercussions of those choices—for the spread of morally deficient character can only make matters worse in the long run. Perhaps the decision not to destroy hundreds of thousands of innocent civilians in Japan, for example, would have led to a much better world today than what we are actually seeing. If there is no way of knowing either way, then isn't our only reasonable option the decision not to do evil that good may come of it?

30. Vanity: A Note on Resolving Morally Ambiguous Cases

An important principle of human knowing is that the higher the level of abstraction on which we think, the greater the certainty we enjoy. As we move towards the realm of the particular (the contingent), matters become less certain and our method becomes more inductive (moving from evidence to explanation) and our conclusions become more or less probable. That is why mathematics enjoys great certainty than biology, for the latter is inductive and investigative. This does not mean that it is impossible to possess certitude in biology; it just means one must work harder to achieve it—mathematicians don't require labs, only a pencil and paper. Ethics follows the same pattern. There are universal principles that are quite certain, but as we move to the realm of the particular, matters become somewhat murkier. It does not mean that it is impossible to determine what the truth of the matter is in such cases; it just means that truth is much more difficult to acquire, more distinctions have to be made, circumstances have to be taken into consideration, etc.

Consider the objections some of my students have raised in class about the bodybuilder. Many will defend the possible reasonableness of the bodybuilder's actions: "What if he is doing it because he just wants to look nice? What's wrong with wanting to look good? Etc." The objections raised are good ones and they help illustrate a point. When an action is not intrinsically evil, such as lifting weights, it becomes a matter of prudence to determine under what circumstances the action becomes morally questionable. Let's liken this to a meter that contains three zones, a zone of reasonableness, a clear zone of unreasonableness, and a zone of ambiguity in which we are not sure whether the act is reasonable or not. It is reasonable to assume that we all agree to the following:

A)Reasonable Zone (health-life)	(B)Zone of Ambiguity	(C) Unreasonable Zone (vanity)
A man works out because he had spent 3 months in a hospital bed recovering from surgery and his muscles have atrophied. He needs to strengthen certain muscles that have not been used in a while. He is required to work out 4 days of the week, for 1 hour or so for each day he is at the gym.		A man spends a large portion of his income on certain drinks that will build muscle, spends a great deal of time at the gym in order to build 18 inch biceps, 56" chest, wants to look "notorious" and impress the girls, looks at himself in the mirror all the time, etc. His body has become the center of his own existence. Little else matters in his life except looking "buff" and powerful.

What my students were essentially arguing is that there is a zone of ambiguity. What if he does not fall into Zone C, but not Zone A either?

A)Reasonable Zone (health-life)	(B)Zone of Ambiguity	(C) Unreasonable Zone (vanity)
	A man bodybuilds as a sport, which is an aspect of leisure (a basic intelligible human good). He does not spend	

	inordinate sums of money on himself, does not spend an inordinate amount of time on himself, but also wants to "look good" for others, even looking "buff"	

This is a zone of ambiguity. If bodybuilding is not intrinsically wrong (as some actions are), then it is very difficult to determine when or whether someone operating in Zone B has crossed into Zone C.

A)Reasonable Zone (health-life)	(B)Zone of Ambiguity	(C) Unreasonable Zone (vanity)

	X
	
	X
	    X
	          X
	     X	

This is an illustration of how moral matters become murky as we descend to the level of the particular. It does not mean that morality is all relative—it is absolutely true that one ought to act in accordance with reason; it is just that sometimes determining what contravenes reason is not always so easy. It's like the virtue of temperance. How much is too much alcohol? One drink? Two drinks? Perhaps it is comparable to trying to determine when a house, which is in the process of being built, actually comes into being. At what point is it a house? When the foundation has been laid? When the roof shingles have been laid? When it has been fully bricked? When the drywall is in place? This is genuinely ambiguous.

Morality is much simpler when we are dealing with actions that are intrinsically wrong. That's why we spend a great deal of time trying to determine whether certain acts are intrinsically wrong. Is lying intrinsically wrong? Is giving someone a lethal injection intrinsically wrong? Is capital punishment intrinsically wrong? If an action is intrinsically wrong, then no circumstance can justify the action, that is, no circumstance can make the act reasonable.

A Note on Ultimate Ends

But what's wrong with vanity? When someone says: "So and so is vain", they are basically saying that the person is too preoccupied with himself or herself. What this boils down to is the question: "What constitutes a good or morally noble life?" This is why beginning with Aristotle's *Nichomachean Ethics* is a good idea when teaching morality, and not a rigorous Natural Law approach. The *kalon*, the morally beautiful or noble, is a life ordered towards the highest things. So, for Aristotle, contemplation of the highest things is the highest activity in man, because intellect is the highest power (knowing is the highest activity). So a good life is ordered to a good end, and the best end is the contemplation of the highest things—for Aquinas and Augustine, this translates into the "highest thing" or highest being, which is God. So the purpose of human life is the eventual contemplation of God as He is in Himself (that was how Europe in the Middle Ages re-interpreted the Greeks, i.e., Aristotle and Plato). The rest of the virtues are ordered to that end. This differs from the Epicureans who believed that pleasure alone was the ultimate end.

So, I think this question gets resolved when we look at what a person's ultimate end is. If his ultimate end is pleasure, for example the pleasure he takes in himself, his looks, or that others admire him, etc., if that is his ultimate end and everything else in his life, all his resources, are ordered to that end, then he has made himself the center of his own existence. Vanity means "worthless", a waste, so to speak. So take the case of someone who has made pleasure his ultimate end and everything else is ordered to procuring this pleasure, i.e., total preoccupation with his body and looks. I'm sure you would agree that this is a twisted and disordered life. It is a waste, if and only if there is a higher end to human life than mere pleasure.

Now, take the case of someone who has not made himself and his own pleasure the ultimate end of his life. Take the case of someone who may not even be "religious" per se, but who lives for the common good of the civil community (let's say he has no religious convictions, for whatever reason). In this case, he orders his life, his emotions, his individual actions, in accordance with this end. And let's say he decides he wants to work out, he wants to look good. He's probably not going to want to invest as much as the hard core bodybuilder we looked at in the previous paragraph would be willing to invest—he simply can't afford the time, because there is more to his life than his body. Since his end in life is the common good of the civil community, his particular vocation in life reflects that. Let's say he's in medical research, and on the side he coaches little league baseball or hockey, he's got a wife and kids, etc., In other words, his actions reflect his ultimate end, which is the common good of the civil community. There is nothing wrong with him working out to be fit, healthy, and even wanting to look good. But as for wanting 18" biceps and bulging muscles in order to impress others, that would be unlikely in his case, because it does not fit with the overall commitment of his life. Such a desire is incongruent with his overall end in life. His primary desire is the common good. He doesn't have the time to devote to himself to achieve a super muscular body. If his end was himself, his own looks, then he'd make the time for that. But he does not.

Now, can we compare these two lives? Can we compare their ends? Can we say that the first guy who has made pleasure and self his ultimate end, is less noble than the guy who has made the common good his ultimate end? I would argue we can. I would argue that there is an intelligible structure to human existence, that is, there is a determinate nature that we refer to as "human nature", and a morally good life accords with that nature. A life that makes the self and its own pleasure the ultimate end is less than fully human—in other words, there is more to human nature than the sensitive appetites. And there are people who live less than fully human lives.

Now it's hard or next to impossible to draw the line that indicates where reasonable concern for one's looks ends and unreasonable concern for one's looks begins. Unreasonable concern for one's body is vanity. It's the overall end in life that determines what is reasonable. If the intelligible human goods include "harmony between oneself and others" (friendship), as well as the common good of the civil community, then a good life will include the pursuit of these. A good life will put higher goods in higher priority (i.e., justice will be more important than pleasure). The common good of the civil community is a higher good than my body. The body is good and looking good is a good thing, and wearing makeup is good as well—it is not necessarily vain. But a person can become too preoccupied with his or her complexion. What counts as "too" preoccupied? That's hard to say. But, if there is no network of intelligible human goods, but only one good, namely pleasure (which is what hedonism believes), then there is nothing wrong with a life that is centered around looking good and feeling good. Nothing at all. In fact, a life devoted to the common good would appear as a waste of time, as something irrational, if and only if there is one good, namely pleasure and self- promotion. And that is why some people look upon the lives of others and just can't understand why they do what they do—i.e., some people wonder why others care about what goes on in other countries, or why others care about injustices overseas, or that people in other countries are lacking proper medical care, etc.

So I think it all depends on the overall framework of what you regard as the ultimate end of human life, and the answer to that question will depend on your understanding of human nature.

31. St. John the Baptist

I'd like to make a few points on the basis of three significant events in the New Testament that have to do with St. John the Baptist. The first event is the reaction of John in the womb of his mother, Elizabeth; the child leapt for joy in Elizabeth's womb upon hearing Mary's greeting. There is so much meaning packed into this brief event; John reacts to the presence of Mary, the mother of Jesus. Elizabeth was filled with the Holy Spirit upon receiving Mary's greeting, and John reacts to the sound of her voice.

Consider how many others in Egypt, for example, were filled with the Holy Spirit, without really understanding the significance of what was happening to them, all as a result of simply being in the presence of Mary when she was in Egypt with Joseph. This is important to think about, because so many people are under the impression that in order to really witness to Christ, you have to "preach" to people and convince them of the truth of certain propositions and even convert them to your "religion". But Mary simply greeted Elizabeth and as a result her cousin was filled with the Holy Spirit, and the reason is that Mary was filled with the Holy Spirit, for she had just conceived by the power of the Holy Spirit. And what happened to Elizabeth affected the child in her womb.

We human beings are not isolated individuals; we influence one another in ways we are often completely unaware of. As a teacher, I have to continue to remind myself of this, because we can get so caught up in what we teach, in the curriculum, as if the knowledge we impart to our students is the most important thing in the world. The fact is our students will forget most of it, but students do not forget who were to them. As a parent, or a teacher, a priest, whatever it is we do, the most important and most fundamental thing we can do is to pray often and grow in the Holy Spirit, to be increasingly filled with the Holy Spirit, and that very fact will influence others subconsciously.

The next event in the life of John the Baptist occurs later, when he is baptizing in the Jordan. The gospel of Matthew tells us that John wore a garment of camel's hair and a leather belt around his waist, and his food was locusts and wild honey. In other words, he lived a life of austerity, like the prophet Elijah who also wore a haircloth and a belt around his waist. And Jesus referred to John as the greatest prophet: "...truly I tell you, among those born of women there has arisen no one greater than John the Baptist" (Mt, 11, 11).

John was called by God from the womb, as it was the case for Jeremiah: "Before I formed you in the womb I knew you, before you were born I set you apart; I appointed you as a prophet to the nations" (Jer, 1, 5). If this is true for the prophet Jeremiah, how much more for John, the new Elijah who reacted in the womb to Mary's greeting. There is no doubt these events underscore the evil of abortion. What this shows is that abortion is more than the destruction of a developing human life; it is the destruction of a mission, one that is bound to influence countless others and affect the world in ways that we cannot begin to imagine. Just think of how many people you have influenced in your own life; you and I are only aware of a fraction of it, and part of the joy of heaven will be to see just how many people have been influenced by our life and character. The destruction of one irreplaceable mission is impossible to comprehend in all its details, but imagine 56 million unborn children every year, called by God from the womb, destroyed by abortion. We really are at war; and it is a spiritual war, without any doubt.

John the Baptist's penitential life is very important. I find it amazing that I have to explicitly teach senior grade twelve students the difference between reason and emotion and that a humanly good life is guided not by emotion (i.e., the passions), but by reason, and that to allow yourself to be governed by your passions is to live like brutes. This is a real revelation to many of them; and these are very bright kids who study calculus, physics, and who are going on to study engineering, etc. And what is obvious to anyone who drives a car is how impulsive so many people are these days; so many people have little control over their passions and impulses—so many adults, that is. They drive dangerously because they are impatient, they cannot tolerate any kind of delay of gratification—this is especially evident on bright and sunny days. As a culture, we don't teach this anymore; on the contrary, we counsel our youth to do what they're passionate about—to follow their passions, their dreams. The only students I have who live penitential lives are my Muslim students, who every year complete a rigorous one month fast for Ramadan, and my students are always faithful; they eat nothing from sun up to sun down. It is for this reason that they have a profound interest for things spiritual, moral, and intellectual, and very little interest in the sensual.

It is a spiritually healthy thing to practice some sort of penance or sacrifice every day, because our greatest enemy is a disordered love of self, and that love of self is insidious. It is subtle, and it destroys the moral and spiritual life, and this life is a preparation for eternal life, as John's life was a preparation for the Messiah. The only way to keep that love of self from becoming the monster that will destroy our moral and spiritual life is to practice, every day, some kind of penance, that is, some kind of sacrifice. The more we conquer this disordered love, the greater will be our awareness of God's presence at the deepest level of the self and what His will for us really is. Like Elijah on the mountain, the more sensitive will we be to the gentle breeze that brushes across our face, so to speak, which he sensed was the presence of God (1 K 19, 11-13).

And finally, John speaks out against Herod, who married his brother's wife Herodias—she left her husband to marry Herod. This was contrary to the Mosaic Law, which forbids the union of a man with his brother's wife while the brother is still living. John publically disgraced them by speaking out against their union, and he was put to death for doing so. In other words, John loved the law of God more than he loved his own life.

I have always been struck by John's tremendous courage. He reminds me of the prophet Nathan, who confronted David for his sin of taking Bathsheba as his wife, after having her husband moved to the front lines of battle so that he would be killed. Nathan stood before the king and called him on it; that took tremendous courage.

This is precisely what is missing today in the world: courageous leadership; prophets with guts. It seems everyone is capitulating to the pressures of political activists of the politically correct sort, especially university administrators; very few want to speak their minds for fear of reprisal; very few are willing to stand out and risk ridicule or a loss of revenues. But John spoke out against a marriage, an unlawful one. And such a thing is very much worth speaking out against, because marriage is the most fundamental institution: the family is the basic unit of society, and it is here where human beings are most profoundly influenced. The most basic human need is to be loved, to know that you are loved, and the two most important people in a child's life is his or her mother and father. When that relationship interrupted, the children of that marriage are profoundly affected. Children think egocentrically, which is natural for a child. This means that if daddy left me, then it is only because there is something wrong with me. Children idealize their parents—their parents are gods, they cannot do wrong. So, the child always blames himself or herself for any kind of abuse, or neglect, or marriage break up, and the child will internalize this, and these scars last a lifetime. Marriage is so important that it is the model used in Scripture to illustrate the relationship between God and Israel, and in the New Testament, Jesus and his Church: Christ the Bridegroom, and the Church as his Bride.

And so, at the beginning of John's life is a message about the sanctuary of the womb, and at the end of his life is a message about the sacredness of marriage. Between these two points, John's life is a message about this life as a preparation for eternal life, and we prepare the way of the Lord and make straight his path in our own life not by indulging in the pleasures of this world, but by prayer and penance and faithfully carrying out the mission that was given to us from God before he formed us in the womb.

32. Zacchaeus

I recall the first time I saw the show *Dragon's Den*. I didn't like it at all. I thought: "Who are these arrogant people sitting on their thrones, looking down their noses at others struggling to make a living?" I don't think that anymore. I think I might have been too quick to pronounce judgment. They might actually do a lot of good; they certainly take big risks by investing in young entrepreneurs, they provide employment, and it is people like that who enable the economy to expand and flourish. And there's a lot of know about business and economics, and many of us just don't know a whole lot about these things, and instead of admitting it and reserving judgment, we make quick and unfounded inferences on the basis of scanty evidence.

I think there has always been a general and unfounded prejudice against the rich that is probably rooted in envy. But this gospel is particularly interesting for the wealthy. Zacchaeus is a wealthy man, and he was well hated; he was a tax collector, and tax collectors were generally a well hated group of people. The fact of the matter is that we need not be envious of the wealthy. They are just as restless as any of us. In fact, cognitive psychologist Daniel Kahneman points out that there is no correlation between an increase in wealth and an increase in happiness. Once a person is making over a certain amount each a year, his or her happiness will plateau, no matter how much their wealth increases.

But this story of Zacchaeus reveals just what the key to happiness really is, and it holds the key to a more just world. We live in a profoundly unjust world, and everyone seems to have a solution to the world's problems, whether that's raising taxes, lowering taxes, more socialism or a more libertarian society, more education, better education, free education, more technology, a central world government, etc. But none of these are the answer. What will transform people is right here in this story, and it all begins with a desire that is conceived in the heart of Zacchaeus. He desires to see who this Jesus is. But Zacchaeus was short; he couldn't see through the crowd of people. At this point he has a choice: he's got his money, he's got employment, so he can turn around and go home. But he doesn't. He climbs a sycamore tree. That's quite an effort.

The Old Testament makes it very clear that God waits for us to take the first step: "If you return to him with all your heart and all your soul, then he will return to you and hide his face from you no longer" (Tobit 13, 6). The book of Wisdom says that Wisdom anticipates those who desire her: "Whoever gets up early to seek her will have no trouble but will find her sitting at the door" (Wis 6, 13-14). Jesus is the wisdom of God made flesh. And so he should know who has taken a step towards him, that is, who desires to see him. And he does. He calls out: "Zacchaeus, come down quickly, for today I must stay at your house."

At this point, Zacchaeus could have said "No. I don't know you. This would be an inconvenience." But he doesn't. He receives him with joy. But notice what takes place afterward. Zacchaeus was utterly transformed; he became a completely different person. There's something about this Person, Jesus of Nazareth, who brought about this radical transformation. Before, Zacchaeus loved money, as most people do; that's what he lived for. Money was more important to him than his own character—we know that from his own mouth, for he was guilty of extortion. In other words, he was an unjust man. But that all changed immediately. He says: "Behold, half of my possessions, Lord, I shall give to the poor, and if I have extorted anything from anyone I shall repay it four times over."

The poor have come to mean more to him now than his possessions only because Jesus means more to him than his money. Charity has taken root in his heart; he remembers the extortions he might have committed in the past, and has resolved to repay them fourfold. That's an astounding transformation. What did he suddenly receive that would make him so indifferent to his money? Clearly something of much greater value than his wealth. There's a light within him now that wasn't there before. He immediately recognizes that no matter how much wealth he accumulates from this point onwards, it will not bring him anything close to what he now has, all as a result of receiving Jesus into his home.

All we have to do is receive Jesus into our homes. Consecrate our home to him. Give every aspect of our lives to him, receive him completely into our lives, and then nothing else, unrelated to this, will matter. We won't need anything else; we won't desire anything else for ourselves; our happiness will lie in the happiness of others. Like Zacchaeus, we will be moved to think of other people, those who suffer, the poor, the sick, the mentally ill, and those we have caused to suffer, and so we will be moved to repent and make up for the wrong we've done to others, and our happiness will lie in living not for ourselves, but for others, that they might know the joy of having received Jesus into their homes. This is what Pope Francis was saying in the interview that the media tried hard to distort—and succeeded, because most people don't like to read anything more than headlines. He wasn't saying that he is liberal on morality or that life issues are not important; rather, he was saying that when you know the joy of having received Christ into your life, a morally good life will automatically flow out of that. What people need is not ideology, nor a set of moral doctrines to live by, they need a Person, and the Truth became a Person. Salvation is a Person, not an idea, not a government program, but a Person, the Person of Christ.

33. Knowledge and Purity

A friend of mine recently said Mass for an elementary school and during the homily he asked the young students to provide him with one word that they think best describes the Mass. One girl raised her hand to say: "Mass is going to Church"; another said "Mass is praying to God", etc. He assured them that their answers were true, but he reminded them that he was looking for one word that would best describe what the Mass is. One young grade six boy raised his hand and said: "Sacrifice". "What do you mean?" asked my friend. He said: "God does all this stuff for us, but what can we offer to God in return? We have to give something back to God, but we have nothing good enough to give Him. So he sent Jesus to us so that we might have something to give to God."

Needless to say, my friend was quite taken aback. "I want to talk to you after Mass", he said. But the boy was not finished: "It's like a ladder. God came down on a ladder, and Jesus is the ladder that we use to get back to God."

Recently I discovered that a friend of mine, a colleague in teaching, has experienced the same phenomenon that I have experienced over the years when teaching the lowest grades of high school students (grades nine and ten). Both of us tend to discuss more theology and at a much loftier level with our grade nine and ten students than we ever do with our grade twelve students. Why is it that we both sense that grade nine and ten students have a greater capacity to appreciate deeper and loftier theological ideas than the more "sophisticated" grade twelve students? And how does one explain the profound theological response of a grade six child to a simple question about the nature of the Mass?

I believe the answer lies in a very real connection between purity and knowledge, in particular the intellectual gifts of the Holy Spirit (wisdom, knowledge, and understanding). My younger students have a greater innocence and purity than most of the senior students of the school. This is especially true of the grade six boy who understood so much about the Mass. St. Thomas points out that lust, which is inordinate sexual desire, produces four offspring, two of which are related to the intellect: lust darkens or clouds the mind and it destroys counsel, which is an important part of prudence. Gluttony (dainty eating) also dulls the intellect and leads to a loss of interest in things spiritual and intellectual, according to Aquinas.

To clearly explain the intimate connection between purity and knowledge, however, is not easy. I believe that a deeper glance at the hierarchy of being within the physical universe provides a clue. At the lowest end of the hierarchy we find the mineral level, which is characterized by physical and chemical change. When non-living matter reacts with other elements, chemical changes may occur, and when these take place, both chemicals cease to be what they are and become something else entirely, for example, hydrogen and oxygen cease to be what they are and become an entirely different kind of substance, namely water.

But higher still is the vegetative level, that is, the level of living things. The most fundamental activity at this level is nutrition, in which the living thing will take non-living matter into itself, transforming it into living matter. As a result, the living thing grows. What is different about this nutritive activity from the previous (chemical change on the mineral level) is that the plant remains what it is while the minerals cease to be what they are. Water or salts from the soil, for example, which are non-living matter, when incorporated into the plant are transformed into living parts of a living whole. The plant has a greater stability and its activity is immanent, as opposed to the merely transeunt activity of non-living things.

Higher than the vegetative is the animal level, characterized by the activities of sensation and sense appetite. At this level, a material singular thing acts upon the senses of the animal, for example, a surface hot to the touch, or light that acts upon the retina, or sound waves that act upon the ear drum, etc. But sensation is more immanent than nutrition; for sensation is a knowledge of material singulars; the animal knows something outside of itself without ceasing to be itself and without changing the object of its perception. For example, seeing an apple does not change the apple, or hearing a cat in the bushes does not change the cat, and neither does smelling the spruce tree change the tree.

The highest level within the physical universe is of course the human level, which is characterized by a different kind of knowing, an intellectual knowing and willing. Intellectual knowledge is not limited to a knowledge of material singulars, but opens up onto a world of universals (concepts, ideas). The human person is capable of knowing the natures of things, what they are in themselves. We also apprehend the very existence of the thing whose nature we come to know, and we are able to reason, on the basis of those universal ideas, to what we do not know directly, but indirectly. An important point to note is that animals only know material singular things, and only insofar as these have a reference to themselves. Brute animals do not contemplate, nor do they appreciate beauty. They are not interested in the masterworks of Greek or Latin literature, for example. One day I came home to discover that the spine of my 1941 Random House edition of *The Basic Works of Aristotle* had been chewed up. There must have been some leather in the cover that my dog found appealing, but there was nothing about the content of the book that was of any interest to her. The human person, on the other hand, can know things as they are in themselves, their natures and principles, and the human person can will the good of other human persons without any reference to the self.

Now, there is a hierarchy within each level of the hierarchy of being. Certain substances are more stable than others; certain plants are more beautiful than others, and who would doubt that a horse is superior to a worm. The lowest in each hierarchy is near in perfection to the highest in the level below it.

Man's purpose is to exist most fully, and he achieves that by coming to know and love the highest things for their own sake—or the highest being. The lower he is, the more he approaches the level of the beasts, and when he lives at such a low level, almost everything he cares to know about is ultimately for the sake of himself. The criminal, in some ways like a brute animal, lives by destroying others for the sake of his own preservation. And although some are not criminals willing to destroy others, they might be better compared to parasites that live on their hosts without benefiting or killing them. At the highest end of this level is the saint who willingly gives his life so that others may live and that God may be loved.

Now there is a point in human development, at the end of childhood and at the beginning of adolescence, at which the young person has achieved a certain level of intellectual maturity. At this point, there remains in such a person the purity of childhood, and the eyes of such youngsters do not have the degree of self-reference that they will have as they proceed through adolescence. With the onset of sexual maturity, the mode of perception and knowing of senior high school students, generally and for the most part— there are exceptions—, becomes somewhat more self-referenced. He or she will begin to see others and evaluate them on the basis of what they can do for him or her sexually or romantically.

This is a necessary stage of human development, to be sure, but what happens here is that childhood and its accompanying purity are left behind. The heart is not as selfless, and so the mind's activity is less oriented to being for its own sake, being as it is in itself, and it is being that lights the mind. The greater the disposition to refer reality to the self, the more diminished is the light that illumines the interior of the intellect. This movement towards the self is a turning towards the bestial, and with that lowering comes a decreased ability to know for the sake of knowing and to love for the sake of the other, not the self. There is, thus, a corresponding loss of interest in things spiritual.

Perhaps this explains the strange phenomenon of being more able to discuss loftier theological ideas with young grade nine and ten students than with those in later adolescence—let alone adults thoroughly immersed in the world. The purity of childhood is a quality we are obligated to re-capture: "Blessed are the pure in heart; for they shall see God" (Mt 5, 8). After adolescence, the human person has to re-learn that selfless way of seeing the world, but he can only do so by becoming selfless, that is, through the virtue of purity. This can be seen as a return to what is best in childhood: "Unless you change and become as little children, you will never enter the kingdom of God" (Mt 18, 3).

34. Dogmatism, Uncertainty, and the Importance of an Open Mind

It is not easy to define the fundamentalist. Fundamentalism, for me at least, is an interesting phenomenon from the point of view of the theory of knowledge. What Protestant Christian fundamentalists seem to have in common is a literal interpretation of scripture, but this too may not be entirely accurate. Some fundamentalists hold that hermeneutics is very important, that is, careful interpretation that takes the language and historical context of scripture seriously. I often refer to "Catholic fundamentalists", but clearly and unambiguously articulating just what that means is not easy. I think I can safely say, however, that all fundamentalists are dogmatists.

Recently a friend of mine asked: "Should protestant fundamentalists be faulted for believing the plain language of the Bible rather than the more thoughtful and nuanced Catholic apologetics?" My best answer at this point is that I think people should be faulted for giving up their common sense and allowing their need for certainty to override it. Bertrand Russell once said that the demand for certainty is one which is natural to man, but is nevertheless an intellectual vice. He argued that "to teach how to live without certainty and yet without being paralysed by hesitation is perhaps the chief thing that philosophy, in our age, can do for those who study it".

The older I get and the more I observe, I find that Russell is right to observe that "The whole problem with the world is that fools and fanatics are always so certain of themselves, and wiser people so full of doubts". Very few people today are comfortable with ambiguity, that is, with not-knowing. Many people suffer from a kind of "philosophical autism", a disordered need for closure, a need so great that discussion, debate, patient research, etc., is virtually shut down and opposing points of view are dismissed and ridiculed—people would rather have illusions of knowledge because of the feeling of security that it brings.

But the world is utterly rich in complexity, as a simple glance at the history of the developing taxonomy of physics or psychology makes manifest. In 1911, there were two branches of Astronomy: Astrophysics and Celestial Mechanics. Optics branched off into Theoretical Optics and Spectroscopy, and Acoustics was simply that, nothing more. But by 1970 there were 9 specialties of that branch of Astronomy called Solar-Planetary Relationships, 6 specialties of Planetology, and 11 further Astrophysical specialties, 9 specialties of Acoustics, and 10 specialties of Optics, etc. Consider how much psychology has developed over the past 200 years. There is only one human nature, but there are various schools of psychology: Structuralism, Functionalism, Behaviorism, Gestalt Psychology, Psychoanalysis (Freud), etc., and there are different perspectives, such as the evolutionary perspective, the biological perspective, the cognitive perspective, the humanistic perspective, the psychodynamic perspective, the sociocultural perspective, etc., and there seem to be far more branches of psychology now than there were when I first studied this back in the 80s: Clinical psychology, Counselling psychology, Educational psychology, Developmental psychology, Personality psychology, Social psychology, Environmental psychology, Experimental psychology, Industrial/organizational psychology, Cognitive psychology, Health psychology, Sport psychology, Forensic psychology, etc. In other words, reality is utterly rich in complexity and can be studied from various different angles and from innumerable starting points.

Moreover, knowledge is very hard to achieve, which makes life all the more interesting and exciting. A recent discussion with my students on certain questions in the area of virtue ethics bore this out. The more abstract and general the level of discussion, the greater the certainty, but as we descend to lower levels of abstraction (i.e., the realm of the particular and contingent), things become murkier and much more opaque. Again, this does not mean there is no "truth" on this level; rather, it means that truth is much harder to uncover. General principles are always easier to handle than their application to particular situations, which is why mathematics enjoys greater certainty than say history. The lower the level of abstraction on which a science operates, the more inductive and conjectural is the method, and thus the greater the need for testing, which is why there are no labs in math class, but labs in chemistry and lots of sifting through archives in history. A similar pattern is noticeable in ethics. We all agree with the general principle that we ought to exercise reasonable stewardship of our excess riches (liberality), and we agree that people ought to dress modestly, that is, honestly and reasonably. But determining exactly where that line is and when it is crossed is not at all easy to determine. Some argue that tight jeans and yoga pants are immodest, while other students put forth very plausible arguments that such apparel is not at all immodest, but culturally normal and reasonable.

Indeed, there are different cultural norms with regard to dress, and what is immodest here in Canada is not immodest in Africa. If wearing a bathing suit on a beach is reasonable, why is wearing yoga pants on a street only half a mile from the beach unreasonable? When does fundraising in a school setting become excessive? Have we crossed that line at our school? Some put forth persuasive and plausible arguments that we have, while a few students have put forth an equally persuasive and plausible argument that we have not: i.e., one always has a choice to contribute, fundraising has an important educational value, while others point out that fundraising is outside the scope of the school's purpose, and students do not have an unlimited reservoir of coins that they can reach into whenever they are asked, which seems to be almost weekly, and unnecessary pressure is placed on students to donate, etc.

The beauty of the discussion is that it highlights the complexity and opacity involved in plausible reasoning. No one side was absolutely and unambiguously right, and no one was clearly wrong; every point made in class was a very insightful one that increased the plausibility of their side of the issue, and plausible claims just kept piling up. And in many ways, that was a better lesson than the simple deposit of "the right answer". I still don't "know" what the right answer is—regarding modesty and liberality—, although I lean less to one side than I did before we had the discussion. However, it is easy to find an inordinately fervent Catholic who would put an immediate end to the discussion and declare, with great confidence, that the bikini is immodest. No discussion! Clear and evident! Of course, it is far more complicated than that. Perhaps it was next to impossible to find a woman to model the bikini when it first came out—only strippers were willing—, but that does not resolve the issue; in fact, it only begs the question; perhaps the social norm at the time was unreasonably prudish.

It's the complexity and resulting uncertainty that makes science very interesting as well. Reality is always much richer than we currently realize, which is why science continues to develop. Very few good scientists are "dogmatists"; they know that eggs placed in today's "scientific basket" will likely be overturned tomorrow, and thus they have a greater appreciation for the tentativeness of truth. Fundamentalists, of whatever stripe (i.e., Catholic, Protestant, Muslim, Hindu, Jewish, etc.), do not for a minute believe that truth is tentative. In their minds, it is absolute, clear, unchanging, etc. Indeed, in itself, truth is absolute and unchanging, but the "in itself" is an idealization. All we have is truth "as I see it currently", as I have estimated and articulated it, as it appears to me within a limited model consisting of a number of epistemic conditions that were gradually acquired. If what I apprehend is true, then it will endure, it will never be falsified, but how do I know that further data, including rational data such as new insights spawned from new questions posed within different geographic and temporal circumstances, will not arrive on my doorstep next week that renders my current argument—made up of a large set of consistent propositions and premises—inconsistent and far less plausible? It has happened countless times since I began to study philosophy; why would I assume that such a process would suddenly come to an end?

But dogmatists and fundamentalists find that realm of "unknowing" very uncomfortable. And the irony is that God is the unutterable mystery. The increasingly complex taxonomy of all the sciences is testimony to the inexhaustible richness, complexity, and depths of reality, and from a theological point of view, the latter is a sign of the inexhaustible and incomprehensible nature of God, the unutterable mystery who is the source of all that exists. God can never be comprehended (in the sense of fully understood or intellectually circumscribed). The evolution of the universe (13.6 billion years old), the evolution of the planet (4.6 billion years old), the evolution of life, the evolution of science, and the evolution of thought in general, should fill us with wonder, but instead some will rebel against it and demand certainty and stability. There's the congruity between science and religion: both center on mystery, and both require a similar attitude of "unknowing" and openness, an ability to live and breathe within a space of doubt.

My friend finished by asking: "How am I to recognize what is "simply a false or profoundly deficient bit of inhumane ideology and what is the profoundly thoughtful, nuanced word of God?" That is a great question, and I wish I could answer it, but I can't, at least not at this point. It's like asking: How can I recognize what is good science from bad science, or fake news from real news, etc. I don't know. Discerning fake news from genuine news is about learning to be less gullible, learning to reason more critically, becoming very familiar with the fundamentals of logic, etc., but even that isn't enough. I don't think there is a way to discern what is genuine from what is not genuine from the sidelines, so to speak. In other words, there is no formula that one can isolate and use as a standard. One just has to get into the thick of things and deal with the messiness of reality and enjoy the adventure.

There is no "paper" infallibility; scriptural or sacred texts are read and interpreted by limited human beings whose minds are clouded by disordered passion. Although Catholics believe the bible to be the inspired word of God, there is a distinction between a proposition and an assertion, and yet determining what is asserted and what is not is no easy task. Biblical interpretation, like all textual interpretation, is an inductive process, like trying to solve a crime, and it involves both deductive and inductive arguments. It is not and never has been a final and once and for all deal. There has been a development in the Church's understanding and interpretation of Scripture, and that understanding continues to develop in conjunction with new religious experiences, new advancements in science, psychology, and philosophy, among other areas of knowledge.

www.ingramcontent.com/pod-product-compliance
Lightning Source LLC
Chambersburg PA
CBHW030105070426
42448CB00037B/973